MY JOURNEY TO GRANDMA'S MARATHON
HISTORY & HEROES

BY SCOTT KEENAN

Tom,

Thank you for the many years of support!

Best wishes always,

Scott

MY JOURNEY TO GRANDMA'S MARATHON
HISTORY & HEROES

BY SCOTT KEENAN

Published by: Scott Keenan Books

SCOTT KEENAN BOOKS
http://scottkeenanbooks.com

Paperback ISBN: 978-0-578-86866-0
Library of Congress Control Number: 2021908909

Cover photo: Chuck Curtis, Duluth News Tribune (1977)
Scott Keenan handing Garry Bjorklund a glass of water in the inaugural race of 1977.

Cover Artwork by: Angie Simonson, Main Idea Creative

This is a running book of a different kind.
Enjoy my journey.
It was my dream come true!

~ Scott Keenan

Dedication

I am dedicating this book to all the readers
who consider me a friend.

A special thank you to my wife, Carrie, who has shown
countless hours of patience with me over the years.

Enjoy reading about my journey, the history, and heroes of
Grandma's Marathon, and remember, missing a few
facts should never ruin a good story!

Table of Contents

A Special Thank You…

to Grandma's Marathon and the Duluth News Tribune for the use of the many wonderful photos that appear throughout this book.

Introduction

During my race directing career, I surrounded myself with people who were positive and willing to work hard and follow my vision. My goal was to build an extraordinary community race, an event which people of Minnesota's Northland would be proud of for generations to come.

I believe with all my heart that I had the necessary intuition to create a "World-Class Race With Small Town Charm".

I was never satisfied with Grandma's Marathon staying status quo and fought off any negativity from those who saw the work I was doing in a different light. I ignored them and quickly moved on.

My vision included inviting runners from around the world. It was clear to me that we were going to have our own form of the Olympics in Duluth each year. No discussion. No arguments.

My priority was to stage a safe race and it didn't matter the cost. I wanted to have all of the basic necessities which runners expected, fine-tuned and working to perfection. My goal was to have tremendous water stations, highly-organized traffic control, a first-class medical team on the racecourse and at the finish line, and a flawless runner transportation system.

We were going to have fun as well. It was important to have a celebration afterwards - a party with music, dancing and maybe a few cold beers.

My dream was to showcase Grandma's Marathon and our city to the world, and I never wavered.

There were many times I rolled the dice in making important decisions, but I did it with confidence. I went with my gut feelings and my conclusions were always based on what would be best for the runners.

Some people may have looked at me as being stubborn, headstrong or even quick tempered. For me, it didn't make a lot of sense to keep hashing over details or problems for weeks or even months. We had way too much work to do. We needed to move forward.

I was always nervous at the start of the race, watching the clock tick down with thousands of runners beginning to line up. I took one deep breath and started shouting out orders. I was now calm and focused.

Much of our history has been written. Since 1987, we have hosted nine United States National Championships. They were always held in conjunction with Grandma's Marathon and the Garry Bjorklund Half Marathon.

Very few race organizations in the country have invested as much financial resources and staff energy to support elite runners.

The most satisfying part of my job was working closely with volunteers. I truly enjoyed developing a committee structure that empowered them to use their talents and strengths to organize our weekend races.

Many volunteers have become good friends. We always had fun in the planning, but the work was done in a first-class way.

I never wanted to fail. It was my only fear. I couldn't imagine disappointing the runners and sponsors because of something that could have been avoided. For 37 straight years, I had nightmares leading up to the race. It made me work harder each day. I pushed myself to the limit to have success.

I had a great career in the sport that I loved. No regrets, not one. To steal a line from a Frank Sinatra song:

"I faced it all and I stood tall and I did it my way."

Enjoy the book. It is from my heart.

CHAPTER 1

The Beginning

I'll start my story in 1971, during my senior year at Duluth Central High School. Central was founded in 1892, in the center of our downtown. It is a beautiful three-story building built of Lake Superior brownstone, which features a majestic clock tower that you can see and hear from blocks away.

Ricky Brown and I had just skipped study hall to make a telephone call to Eugene, Oregon. There was a payphone in the hallway near the entrance of the cafeteria and I had a pocket full of quarters.

Ricky and I were planning to take a trip to Eugene after graduation to watch Steve Prefontaine run in a track meet at the legendary Hayward Field. This had been a dream of Ricky's for a long time, which eventually became a dream of mine.

I wasn't on the track or cross-country teams, but Ricky was. Somehow, I became friends with many of the runners in my class, although I absolutely had no interest in running.

My desire was to work and save as much money as I could to give me some level of financial independence from my parents. My working career began when I was 9 years old with my paper route, cutting grass in the neighborhood, raking leaves for fifty cents per hour, bringing Kool-Aid to construction sites and shoveling as many driveways as I could in the winter.

Ricky and I didn't know how to find information about when Pre would run. Obviously, there was no Internet back then. So, we dialed the number to the Eugene Chamber of Commerce. When I finally got through to someone, I was so excited I yelled out, "Is this Eugene?" Ricky was in tears laughing so hard.

We made the connection that afternoon but, sadly, we never did make that trip in the spring of 1972.

* * *

After high school graduation, I followed in my dad's footsteps and made a living mainly by painting houses. I earned up to five dollars an hour, which was pretty good money at that time. Painting was a trade I had been involved in since a very young age by cleaning paintbrushes and doing prep work that no one else would do.

Chester Shannon Keenan, 50 percent Irish and 50 percent French Canadian, was a hard-working individual who made sure there was always plenty of food on the table for his wife and four children. I was the second oldest, born on my mother's birthday in 1953. My mother, Mary, was 50 percent Norwegian and 50 percent Swedish, and was a very petite, yet strict, stay-at-home mother who managed all of her kids as we grew up.

It was a good early life with time spent together as a family – agate hunting by the lake, fishing and taking Sunday drives along the North Shore of Lake Superior. We grew up with many friends and cousins to explore with and build tree houses in the nearby woods.

There were difficult, darker times too, which resulted in memories that I've always tried to forget. Often dad would come home after drinking the night away. He'd be angry at the world and very unpleasant to be around.

On these nights, mom would make sure my siblings and I were in bed early, always attempting to protect us from him as best as she could. I remember many times crying myself to sleep, praying that mom and dad wouldn't get divorced.

It was always clear to us that we were not going to stay home for long after high school graduation. We knew we needed to move on quickly and start the next chapter in our lives.

My older brother, Mike, joined the U.S. Navy and got married to a classmate of mine named Brenda. My younger brother, Gary, moved out to the East Coast and worked in the hospitality industry. My sister, Patti, married at a young age, started her own family and daycare business right after high school graduation.

I came home late one night in the fall of 1971, just after graduation, and found all of my belongings on the front porch. I guess I didn't understand the hint my parents gave me when my graduation present was a piece of luggage.

I packed everything in my royal blue Chevy pickup truck with a topper and left. That night and every night for the next two months I slept in the truck, which I had parked in a secluded wooded area by Chester Creek. As winter approached and the weather took a turn for the worse, I was forced to rent a cheap room in downtown Duluth. In February of 1972, I boarded an airplane bound for San Antonio, Texas, to start my next adventure - basic training.

* * *

By tenth grade in high school, the war in Vietnam was becoming less popular every minute of every day. Boys my age were allowed to put their names on a waiting list to join the Minnesota Air National Guard while still in high school, which I did with little hesitation. I certainly didn't want to be drafted and shipped to 'Nam.

I still remember watching the draft lottery on the television at home. The announcer would pull white ping-pong balls out of a wheel like he was drawing the winner of the lottery. During the forty-second draw, they pulled my birthdate. I was sick to my stomach. I thought for sure I'd be sent to Southeast Asia. Luckily, I was instead bound for Lackland Air Force Base.

On the application I completed when signing up for the Air National Guard in tenth grade, I was able to write down my top three areas of interest for training. There were no guarantees I'd get any of them, but my first choice was to be a fire fighter because my neighborhood friend, Marty Paavola, was already serving as one. I felt that would be a good and safe job to have.

Maybe it was a little Irish luck, getting accepted into the Guards and becoming a fire fighter. One thing I know for sure, I was one of the lucky ones who didn’t get sent overseas.

CHAPTER 2

Basic Training

Before leaving home for Lackland Air Force Base my friend, Marty, gave me two important pieces of training survival advice. First, never ever volunteer for anything, and second do everything possible to prevent the sergeants from learning your name.

I was extremely anxious heading to basic training. It was the first time I'd ever flown on an airplane, and I was also going to be living with 49 other airmen from all over the United States.

Upon landing in San Antonio, we were quickly shuttled to the base for haircuts, uniforms and combat boots. We were then escorted to the barracks where 50 of us in our flight would have to find a way to live together in harmony the next six weeks. In many cases that ended up being a challenge.

My haircut was shorter than anyone's, the barber had shaved my hair down to the scalp. My nickname later became 'Baldy' as every ten or so days I received another haircut and, of course, right down to the scalp. I'm not sure what the barber had against me, but it seemed like everyone was allowed to grow his hair out, but not me. As it turned out, many of the other guys were given nicknames as well – 'Pots and Pans', 'Gomer', 'The Clipper', and 'The Latrine Queen' to name a few.

My first morning didn't start out well. 0500 hours, or 5 a.m., came quickly and lights were turned on and the swearing began to the tune of "GET UP YOU LAZY S.O.B.S!" I was so exhausted that I slept through all of the commotion until one of the sergeants kicked my cot over with me on it. I was politely welcomed to Lackland Air Force Base.

Each morning began exactly at 5 a.m. We'd do a quick set of calisthenics and then march to the chow hall. Later in the morning we were required to run a mile in our stiff and uncomfortable black combat boots on a quarter mile red sand track. I ran with fear the first morning, but to my surprise, I beat everyone in my flight, and received accolades from the training instructors (TIs).

I was very thin, 6 feet tall and weighed about 140 pounds. Many of the guys were heavier and smoked. The calisthenics and the running were easy for me, which gave me hope I just might make it through training.

The first mail call came about five days after arriving on the base. One of the sergeants read off last names on the letters and finally called, "KEENAN!" I was excited to get a letter from home, but it wasn't for me. It was for a guy named Gary Keenan from Maple Shade, New Jersey. The sergeant's response was, "There's two of you!" I was almost in tears because I had already broken one of Marty's rules. The TIs now knew my name.

I am sure the Air National Guard basic training was a piece of cake compared to the Army or other branches of the service. It was still a challenge for all of us. The TIs quickly established a tremendous amount of discipline and taught us how to function as a team, not as individuals. We were constantly threatened to be sent back to redo basic training for another six weeks.

Looking back at it now, I realize that basic training was nothing more than a routine with calisthenics, chow, marching, classes, M-16 rifle training, obstacle course training, running, standing at attention for hours and, if you were unlucky, Kitchen Patrol through the late hours of the evening.

* * *

I really started to enjoy running each morning. It was fun to give it my all and improve my time and distance from the second runner. The accolades were still coming in from the TIs and by my second week in Texas, I really felt like I was becoming a runner.

In the third week we started to run with our sister flight group as well – a total of 100 soldiers. I was fortunate to beat their best runner. It was then that I realized that the TIs won bragging rights when they had the fastest runner, and I certainly wasn't planning to let them down.

Lackland had an inter-base track meet scheduled during my fifth week and to qualify to participate you needed to be the best runner in your squadron of 500 men. I ran hard and I won that race. I was now the squadron running representative.

The Lackland Air Force Base track meet was scheduled on our only day off. We were allowed to visit San Antonio, and I was a little upset to miss the outing, but I didn't really have a choice. I had been selected to represent my squadron.

The night before the race, the guys in my flight were strongly encouraged to volunteer to give a pint of blood. Since my blood type is O negative – the universal blood type – I was expected to volunteer. At the time, I didn't realize this was not the smartest thing to do before a race.

It was extremely warm the afternoon of the meet with temperatures in the high 80s. I was scheduled to run the mile race, but the distance was cut to a half mile because of the warm and humid conditions. While a shorter distance might please some people, it was not welcome news to me. I had been "blessed" with slow twitch muscle fibers, more suitable for longer distances. Plus, I had given blood the night before and wasn't feeling the best.

Needless to say, the race didn't go well. I ran as hard as I possibly could and finished a distant fifth place. I wish I would've gone to San Antonio instead.

Later that day, while still feeling down in the dumps about losing the race, I looked up at the sky and saw a couple of B-52 bombers flying over the base. It was a much-needed reality check that while I was losing half-mile races, there were people losing their lives in Vietnam. I was lucky to be where I was.

* * *

During the last week at Lackland Air Force Base, everyone was required to run a sub-8-minute mile. My closest friend at training, Gary Harshall from Pennsylvania, was the slowest runner in our flight. I promised Gary that I would help pace him through the four long laps.

During the run, the TI's were yelling at me with threats to "send me back" for another six weeks if I didn't start running faster. Gary and I tied for last place with 10 seconds to spare.

Everyone in our flight graduated. It was time to move on to our assigned technical schools for further training.

* * *

I headed off to Chanute Air Force Base in Rantoul, Illinois, for firefighting school. Chanute, established in 1917, was decommissioned for all military use in 1993.

My first day in Illinois didn't go well either. I became severely ill and passed out in the latrine and was shipped off to the base hospital for the next three days, missing the very important orientation. Much to my relief, I found out after being released from the hospital that our new training instructors were much more understanding than those in basic training.

Our days consisted of a variety of training exercises with firefighting equipment, classroom work and tests in every area of our studies. We also did a lot of training for structural and crash fires where we wore protective fire-resistant silver astronaut-looking gear. As part of the course, we were required to put out a thousand-gallon jet fuel fire by layering on protein foam.

In addition to formal training, I managed to find a way to make a little cash on the side. When we were given leave on long weekends, many of the guys went home to visit family and girlfriends. They were required to find someone to cover their 4-hour guard duty shift at the barracks and I saw this as a business opportunity, charging $25 per shift.

* * *

There was little opportunity to run during tech school. We were warned to be careful if we left the base and to make sure to stay together in groups, because a number of trainees had been attacked off base.

One evening a bunch of us decided to go to the local bowling alley for pizza and a few beers. I was the only one who decided to actually bowl. After a couple of games, I looked around for my buddies, but they were all gone. Remembering the warning we had received; I ran the fastest I've ever run to get back to the base. I guess that's one way to get in a run.

* * *

Seven weeks went by quickly and before I knew it, I was back home looking for work and a place to live.

CHAPTER 3

Coming Home

According to the most recent census, Duluth, Minnesota, the birthplace of Bob Dylan, has a population of 86,265. It is the western-most U.S. city on the Great Lakes and was founded on mining and timber industries. By 1980, most of the larger companies like U.S. Steel closed their doors.

I have clear memories of going to school at Duluth Central High when certain times of the year the air was so polluted from the steel and other manufacturing plants discharging poisonous black fumes. You could not see one block in front of you. The economy was in a dire plummet and there was a billboard on Interstate 35 that read, "The last one out, please turn off the lights."

Lake Superior is the world's largest freshwater lake by surface area and holds 10 percent of the world's fresh water. It certainly could be described as the greatest of all the Great Lakes. In 1977, the beautiful North Shore of Lake Superior became the roadway to one of the most respected and scenic marathons in the country.

Upon my return from tech school, I shared an old brownstone apartment in Duluth's East Hillside with two friends, Bob Larson and Jay Lee. Bob had a passion for boxing and Kung Fu training. Jay was a fellow runner and a member of the North Shore Striders.

With Bob's help, I was fortunate to find work in the shipping department of Wahl's Department Store. Bob was already employed there. My starting pay was $2.25 per hour.

It was time to start running on a regular basis, so I reconnected with my friend, Ricky Brown, and he became my mentor. Ricky had only one way to run and that was to go fast and for as long as he could each day. We ran on the secluded streets of Duluth during the late evening hours. We ran time trials of every distance on the University of Minnesota Duluth cinder track. We raced ourselves until we collapsed. I never once ran for fun.

My times were improving each week, but in all honesty, I was beginning to dislike running. I remember purchasing a pair of Adidas Roms from Garry Bjorklund at CZ Wilson's Sporting Goods Store in Duluth. The shoes were white with blue stripes and made of thick heavy leather. At the time they were considered one of the best shoes available.

Garry, who was born in Duluth and grew up in nearby Twig, Minnesota, is a legend in Minnesota running and became a 1976 10,000-meter Olympian and a two-time Grandma's Marathon champion. Much of the marathon's early success goes directly to Garry for his persistent ambassadorship. At a national media platform, Garry was once asked to name his favorite marathon and he replied, "Grandma's Marathon! What more could you want in a marathon? It starts in the middle of the woods, runs along the beautiful North Shore of Lake Superior and finishes at a pub." In 1991, we started a half marathon in conjunction with Grandma's and, without a second thought, it was named the Garry Bjorklund Half Marathon.

After I purchased the Adidas shoes, I seriously thought about quitting running and was upset with myself that I spent money on those shoes. On June 26, 1972, Ricky convinced me to run a 3-mile track race on the University of Minnesota Duluth track. Steve Pfingston, the Central High School track and cross-country coach, organized the event. I was reluctant to run but finished third with a time of 17:14.6, which was a 5:45 minutes per mile pace.

This was only my second month of running, if I didn't count the few miles I ran in basic training. Steve and others congratulated me, which seemed confusing to me because I didn't win. It did bring back good memories of those accolades I received in basic training. I didn't quit running and soon began to fall in love with the sport.

CHAPTER 4

North Shore Striders

In the 1960s, across the USA there were many small pockets of young and passionate runners separated only by distance. The common bond between them was the desire to unite and form local running clubs so they could compete in races.

Days, months, and years elapsed, and they slowly came together and were the catalyst for the beginning of America's first running boom.

In this era, running outdoors in the wintry northern climates was an oddity. It was thought you would certainly freeze your lungs from the cold winter air. I have a vivid memory of running with many cotton long sleeve shirts with old worn-out tube socks on my hands. People in cars would often pull up during my runs asking if I needed a ride. At the time, so many people, including my parents, didn't understand I just wanted to run because it made me feel strong.

My favorite time to run was 10 p.m. when vehicle traffic was almost non-existent, and the air seemed so clear and fresh. It was so easy to "blitz" my favorite 10-mile course.

* * *

In March of 1961, Bob Harris, Chuck Bartholomew, Pat Lanin, Glen Gustafson, Jerry Smith, Ron Daws, Everett Luoma and Dick Flipp decided to establish the Minnesota Road Runners Club (MRRC) based in Minneapolis. These eight dedicated runners are responsible for the beginning of organized road running in Minnesota. The group developed a vision and overcame numerous obstacles in pursuit of their goal to elevate running in Minnesota to the national level.

The club became a branch of the National Road Runners Club of America (RRCA), headquartered in New York. RRCA began in 1958 with the mission to promote distance running by organizing competitive races and educating runners about local and national running news.

In 1968, the members of the MRRC created the Twin Cities Track Club. In 1972, the club changed its name to the Minnesota Distance Running Association (MDRA).

It would be fair to say that their efforts were a huge part of a running craze that has now soared in the United States. It would be appropriate to salute and admire the tenacity of these individuals.

Garry Bjorklund, Bill Andberg, Van Nelson, Rick Kleyman, Garrett Tomczak, Steve Hoag, Jeff Reneau, John Cramer, Emily Lanin, Mike Slack and Dr. Alex Ratelle are others who made contributions to Minnesota running. Of course, there are many who I did not give a shout out to, but no disrespect – Thank you for what you have done!

* * *

1968 Photo of the North Shore Striders track club. Pictured left to right: Coach Eleanor Rynda, Steve Lent, Tim McCall, Gordy Gustafson, Warren MacDougall, Dave Jones, Dan Klenow, Garry Bjorklund, Scott Sundquist, Jim Peterson, Rick Peterson, and Bill Westholm.

In 1968, a few years before I found my love of running, one of the nation's small pockets of passionate runners was in Duluth. Eventually a handful of them banded together to form a competitive track and field club led by a 20-year-old collegiate middle distance track athlete, Duluth Denfeld's Dan Klenow.

The club's first meeting was held at UMD in the spring. In attendance were Garry Bjorklund, who ran a 4:05.1 mile in high school, John Cordes a 1:48.7 half-miler and Dave Jones, who excelled in running distances ranging from the mile to the marathon. During that first meeting the club was officially named The North Shore Striders. Klenow was elected president, with Bjorklund, Cordes and Jones chosen to serve as the other officers.

The North Shore Striders' journey spanned 20 years. Numerous transformations occurred through time, but no matter what changed, the club was always organized and governed by runners for runners.

The North Shore Striders budget was basically non-existent. Each athlete had to absorb expenses for travel to compete in Minneapolis and St. Paul where the majority of the meets were held. Everyone chipped in what they could for gas money and survived on homemade sandwiches.

The Striders were successful early, winning the 1968 Junior National 20,000 Meter Championships, held in Duluth on June 20. Bjorklund, a Proctor High School athlete, won the race, defeating the talented Twin Cities Track Club runners. The Striders took the team title by one point, 29 – 28.

* * *

When there is any discussion about pioneers of running in northern Minnesota, the first person often mentioned is Eleanor "Ellie" Rynda who was born in 1932 and grew up on a small family farm in Montgomery, Minnesota.

Ellie received her Bachelor of Science degree from the University of Minnesota and her Master of Arts degree from Michigan State. She was hired by the University of Minnesota Duluth as a Physical Education and Recreation professor and held that position for 30 years before retiring in 1994.

Ellie's accomplishments were many, but one that stands out came in 1968, when she became the first woman in the country to coach men's track and field and cross country at the university level. Ellie also was the founder of the UMD women's Intercollegiate program. She was inducted into numerous halls of fame and received many other recognition awards throughout her career.

I was fortunate to have Ellie as my coach at UMD. She was firm but fair with her athletes. She only wanted each of us to reach the highest level of excellence possible. Many of us had disagreements with her, but as we look back, we were probably wrong most of the time.

While Ellie was not the driving force in the creation of the North Shore Striders, she did play a major role of supporting Dan Klenow and his crazy band of runners. With the blessing of coach Rynda, the Striders were able to use the university's track and training equipment. Her heart was definitely in promoting this sport, and she loved watching people of all ages run.

Ellie, a very religious woman, died on September 7, 2016, at the age of 83. After the funeral, many of us met at a local restaurant and shared stories of our times with her. Rest in peace Ellie, you will never be forgotten.

* * *

The North Shore Striders quickly grew in popularity from the 1968 team win in Duluth, which led the way to recruit other talented Minnesota runners to join the club. On August 24, 1969, a very hot and humid day in Duluth, the Striders once again were on stage competing in the AAU's 15,000-meter senior road race with Rynda as race director.

Garry Bjorklund held off Olympic marathon runner, Ron Daws, and won a second national title in two years with a time of 49:54.0. Ron was clocked at two-tenths of a second slower in 49:54.2.

The North Shore Striders were again team champions, defeating the Twin Cities Track Club by 3 points, 41 – 38.

The following year the Striders' membership grew to more than 20 athletes of varying talents from track sprinters to marathon runners. Club members proudly wore their deep green colored singlets with matching sweat suits showcasing the gold arch embroidered North Shore Striders lettering. The North Shore Striders was now an official and respected competitive running club in the upper Midwest.

On July 11, 1970, the second Sioux Valley Track Club Classic was held at Roberts Stadium in Sioux City, Iowa. The clubs participating were:

- Coronado Track Club (Stillwater, OK)
- Fort Dodge Track Club (Fort Dodge, IA)
- Iowa Striders (Ames, IA)
- North Shore Striders (Duluth, MN)
- Prairie Striders (Brookings, SD)
- Rochester Track Club (Rochester, MN)
- Sioux Falls Track Club (Sioux Falls, SD)
- Southern State Track Club (Springfield, SD)
- University of Omaha Track Club (Omaha, NE)
- Waterloo Track Club (Waterloo, IA)
- Marion-Cleghorn Track Club (Marion, IA)
- Sioux Valley Track Club (Sioux Valley, IA)

The North Shore Striders finished fifth that day, with only a small portion of the club participating.

The North Shore Striders competed in other Minnesota and Wisconsin races such as the Hopkins Raspberry Festival 5-Mile, Steve Smith Memorial 10-Mile Relay Championships, Paavo Nurmi Marathon and other regional races.

* * *

In 1959, late June and through the first week of August, the Duluth Seaway Port Authority created the Portorama Summer Festival, sponsored by the Duluth Jaycees. In the mid-1960s the Portorama was at its peak of popularity with more than 50 events that took place on 11 consecutive days. The highlight of the festival was a parade with approximately 50,000 spectators lining Superior Street in downtown Duluth.

The Duluth News Tribune wrote, "To count all of the men, women and children and even dogs on Superior Street, would be like counting stars in the Milky Way."

The first recorded running road race in Duluth was in 1965, likely during the Portorama festivities. On August 7, 1965, one of the many events during the Portorama was the 15,000-meter open championship road race sponsored by the Twin Ports Track Club. We can probably declare the club was the first organized track and road-racing club in Duluth's history.

According to Pat Lanin who finished ninth that day, the race started on Skyline Parkway near Enger Tower and ran down the steep Duluth hills on a creaking old boardwalk. They continued on West Superior Street and finished in an industrial neighborhood near the famous Aerial Lift Bridge.

The Twin Cities Track Club easily won the team title with Ron Daws from Minneapolis winning in 45:36.5. There were 22 runners, with many from southern Minnesota. There was also a novice 5,000-meter road race with 16 high schoolers competing. Doug Edmonson from Richfield, Minnesota won in 16:24.5. Dan Klenow, the founder of the North Shore Striders, at that time a junior in high school, finished 12th in18:20.

Sadly, the Portorama Festival came to an end in 1969 due to lack of community support and financial difficulties.

CHAPTER 5

Park Point 5-Miler

Dan Klenow truly enjoyed running and loved to compete. It really didn't matter what distance, or where he ran, as long as he could lace up his shoes and go.

The middle-distance runner from Duluth and president of the North Shore Striders had his eyes set on organizing his first road race. Dan, being a track athlete, was looking for a fast course and, with the support of the police department, Minnesota Avenue (Park Point) was the ideal choice.

Park Point, also known as Minnesota Point, is the home to the world's largest freshwater sandbar that separates Lake Superior Bay and the Duluth Harbor. It is a recreational area used by locals and tourists alike. It is enriched with a sand beach stretching 7 miles.

Dan chose the starting line near the beach house and measured a 5-mile out and back course. Dan got his wish – this was probably the fastest 5-mile course in Minnesota. It was flat as a pancake.

In July of 1972, Scott Sundquist, 19, and a recent graduate of Duluth East High School, won the inaugural Park Point 5-Miler. Scott was one of the top runners in northern Minnesota and ran 24:52.

Scott was fast and always pushed me to my maximum. His parents, Norman and Koni, were very kind and supportive to all of his running friends. They always had plenty of food for us to eat after our runs and I remember the old shower in their dark and damp basement where we could clean up after hard workouts.

Scott died of brain cancer on November 3, 1996 at the age of 43. I was asked to give the eulogy, in which I praised Scott's dedication to the sport. He, in so many ways, was responsible for laying the framework for establishing Grandma's Marathon and other local events.

His humor, laughter and love for people are truly missed by friends and loved ones. His ashes were placed on the beautiful shore of Lake Superior along Stony Point.

In April of 1975, Steve Hoag from Hopkins, Minnesota, placed second to Bill Rogers at the Boston Marathon (2:11:54). Three months later, after Steve's world class run, he chose to drive up Old Highway 61 to Duluth to participate in the Fourth Annual Park Point 5-Miler – Steve easily won the race with a time of 24:16, which is still the course record!

On July 18, 1976, Scott Herron of the Duluth News Tribune staff, reported that Chuck Burrows, 27, from Saint Paul, won the Fifth Annual Park Point 5-Miler, beating a record field of 60. Pat Smith (39) of Ely, Minnesota, was the only female participant, placing 56th.

In 2010, Jennifer Houck of Duluth, posted a women's course record time of 27:50, which hasn't been broken.

Over the years the race changed directors numerous times and in 1997, Grandma's Marathon took over. It's become a fundraising event for the Young Athletes Foundation, which is the charitable arm of Grandma's Marathon.

The race now traditionally attracts more than 500 participants annually and is accompanied by a 2-mile walk and kids races.

I have many fond memories of this race, as it became a wonderful running tradition in the Northland. Many would agree that the Park Point 5-Miler was the beginning of road racing in northern Minnesota.

The North Shore Striders went on to host between 15 to18 races per year of all distances – Grandma's Marathon, the Buhl Half Marathon, Spirit Mountain 10-Mile, Moccasin Mike 9-Mile, Greek-a-thon 10K, Smelt Run 6-Mile, and of course the Park Point 5-Miler to name a few.

In the beginning, most races were 50 cents for members of the club and $1 for non-members. In 1977, the inaugural Grandma's Marathon was pricey as we charged $3 per person, but everyone received a bus ride to the starting line in Two Harbors, a free beer and a lightweight red cotton finisher T-shirt.

Some facts about about Dan Klenow:

- Graduated from Duluth Denfeld High School in 1966
- Attended St. John's University in Collegeville, Minnesota, and participated in track and cross country through December of 1968.
- Transferred to the University of Minnesota Duluth in the middle of his junior year.
- Graduated from UMD in June of 1970, with a B.A. in philosophy and a minor in psychology.
- Continued his education at UMD and finished with a sociology degree in 1971-72.
- In 1973 he was accepted at the University of Toledo and graduated with a master's degree in sociology in 1974.
- He was accepted in the PhD Program at the University of Notre Dame and graduated in 1976.
- Dan is currently teaching courses at North Dakota State on terrorism, cyber security, emerging threats, homeland security and social vulnerability.
- He is married to his wife, Anne, and they have two sons, Tom and Nick. Dan still works out four to five days a week lifting weights and taking lengthy walks.

CHAPTER 6

College Bound

In 1972, my friend Ricky Brown took over as president of the North Shore Striders. I was elected president of the club in 1973 and remained the president through 1979. This marked the beginning of my love of organizing running events and helping develop road racing in northern Minnesota.

It would be fair to say I was probably a better organizer than a runner. Throughout my running career, I was hindered with acute lower back and Achilles tendon injuries. In the fall of 1977, I was also diagnosed with exercise-induced asthma. I knew something was seriously wrong when I was unable to run a mile without gasping for air. At that time there were few treatment options from local physicians. It was an awful feeling, and I was scared I would never run again.

When finishing high school in 1971, I never planned to attend college. I was going to make a living with odd jobs and maybe settle in with a painting career. To be honest I really did not have a plan for my future. I disliked the painting trade, as it seemed that breathing all of the paint and lacquer thinner fumes were counterproductive to my lifestyle.

In my own mind I was practicing a healthy diet, but people who knew me were convinced I was a little weird. I consumed a lot of unsalted nuts, wheat germ, fresh and dried fruits, goat cheese and brewer's yeast shakes. I also took daily desiccated liver supplements, reported to boost energy levels, improve digestion, increase immunity and help maintain blood sugar levels.

I was convinced, without any evidence, that Steve Prefontaine was taking desiccated liver tablets. I was looking for a magical formula to become a better runner – to become another Steve Prefontaine.

I finally decided to make some major changes to my life. I wanted to enroll at UMD during the spring quarter of 1973. I was interested in health as my area of studies, but my real desire was to join the track team.

I soon found out there was a major obstacle. My ACT scores were too low. The admissions office originally refused my entrance application, but I wasn't going to give up. I eventually negotiated a deal where the school could choose the liberal education classes for me and I would promise to pass all of them with good grades, otherwise I would be dismissed.

I enrolled and coach Rynda accepted me on the track team. A new chapter in my life was about to begin.

* * *

Coach Rynda entered me into the 6-mile race during my first collegiate track meet on April 7, 1973. The upperclassmen and the faster distance runners were entered in the 3-mile. Even though I was almost 20, I was a freshman and my more experienced teammates called me a puppy. I had to earn my stripes to become a true Bulldog.

I had never run more than three miles on the track before and never ran in high school. Now, in only my 11th month of running, I was competing in varsity track for my hometown university – in the 6-mile race, nonetheless.

Mile 1 – 5:19.5
Mile 2 – 10:50.3
Mile 3 – 16:31.0
Mile 4 – 22:20.0
Mile 5 – 28:11.7

And my finishing time was 33:50.5. My fastest 3-mile time before this race was 17:14.6. I was exhausted, but happily surprised that I averaged a little over 5:38 minutes per mile.

After the race, my Achilles tendons were severely strained. I was an extreme toe runner and racing with spikes for 24 laps certainly did damage. The following week I ran another 6-mile race and basically limped the whole distance to a disappointing time of 34:59.0.

I now spent a lot of my spare time in the training room in the ice bath for 18 minutes. Don "Doc" Roach was the athletic trainer and did everything he could to get me through the long season. It was difficult to train and extremely painful to compete in races.

I went on to compete in two three-mile races with a best time of 15:59.5. I finished track season running the 6-mile at the conference meet in 33:26.0, which was my best time and a little over 5:36 minutes per mile. While I ended on a high note, it was a very painful season.

I held up my end of the deal with the admissions office, passing all of my classes. My probation period was lifted. I had finally earned my stripes and became an official UMD Bulldog.

* * *

It took me eight years to earn a Bachelor of Applied Science degree from UMD in May of 1981. I paid cash for every credit, refusing to go into debt with student loans. When I needed more money, I went back to work full-time. I was always very good at saving money for what I wanted.

Ever since I was nine-years old working on a paper route, I collected silver mercury dimes. My dad and everyone he knew

Scott Keenan, a proud UMD Cross Country runner.

saved them for me. By1980, I had a large jar full of those dimes, and I sold them for two dollars each when the silver market was at its highest. I used that money for one year of tuition and living expenses.

I didn't attend my college graduation. In fact, I never told anyone I finished college. When dad finally found out he asked to see my diploma. He kept it and framed it for me. My dad never expressed many positive emotions towards me, but at that moment

I knew he was proud. I had graduated from college and earned a teaching degree.

To this day, the proudest accomplishment of my life was graduating from UMD.

CHAPTER 7

Going West

On September 6, 1973, Marty Paavola, Roger Johnson and I left Duluth to take a four-week vacation to explore the western United States. Marty had an older tan colored Ford camper truck, which barely slept three. It was equipped with a small double burner propane stove, tiny sink and a homemade wooden table. I was 20 and Marty and Roger were 22.

We each had $600 cash with no credit cards. During the trip we kept placing $20 in our community expense bucket. The money was mainly used for food, gas and purchasing used tires. The average price of gas in 1973 was 38.5 cents per gallon.

Roger became a close friend and was my fishing partner on many trips to the Boundary Waters Canoe Area in northern Minnesota. I met him through his friendship with Marty. Both were in the same surveying classes at the Duluth Vo-Tech, which later became Lake Superior College. Roger had a bright red Afro, and was a deep thinker, or maybe he could have been considered a 1970s philosopher.

What I remember most about Roger is his contagious laugh that would make everyone smile. I am certain that Roger never had an enemy in his life. He did smoke, but he was always very considerate about it when he was around others.

Marty was medium height, had blonde hair and was a tremendous athlete in all sports. He was captain of his high school swim team, played semi-pro baseball after high school and later became a black belt in Uechie Rue Karate. Marty was a tough guy and on numerous occasions helped me when I found myself in difficult situations. Marty always had my back and I'm extremely grateful for our lifelong friendship.

The Paavola family and the Keenan family lived three houses apart on West Arrowhead Road in the Kenwood Neighborhood.

My second quarter at UMD was on temporary hold. In fact, all three of us were taking a little break so we could make our 12-state journey out west a reality.

My dream to meet Steve Prefontaine was in the forefront of my mind as we stayed in Sioux Falls, South Dakota, during our first night. Marty and Roger were quite aware that our trip was leading to Eugene, Oregon. They were almost as excited as I was.

During our trip we showered at some YMCAs, but mostly crashed at athletic facilities at colleges and universities along the way. Our record for getting in was almost perfect as we were only tossed out once. We cooked our own food to save money, but on occasion treated ourselves at a restaurant for a hearty breakfast.

Our trip took us to the Black Hills and Badlands of South Dakota. We also spent an afternoon checking out Mount Rushmore. Our trip continued to Deadwood and Yellowstone National Park to see Old Faithful.

We spent a few days exploring Cody, Wyoming, and the surrounding area. One night we witnessed a huge bar fight and made sure we stayed far away. We felt a little out of place as the only ones wearing baseball caps instead of cowboy hats.

The next day we took a leisurely four-hour drive to Bozeman, Montana, a southern town in the Big Sky State. It was a small town but was surrounded with beautiful views of the mountain ranges. That evening we found a bar that had a country music band playing. After a few refreshments, Roger and I approached the lead singer and told him, "We have the Minnesota Kid with us. He's one of the best harmonica players in the Midwest."

Marty joined the band for the rest of the set. He was a smashing hit.

Our trip then took us to Seattle where we went directly to the Space Needle and later we drove 60 miles to Olympia, Washington.

* * *

In May of 1984, I returned to Olympia to watch the first U.S. Women's Marathon Olympic Trials. There were 238 starters, with Joan Benoit winning in 2:31:04, just 17 days after arthroscopic knee surgery.

During the trials the women were housed in dormitories at Saint Martin's University. I was granted an official credential allowing me to be in the commons area where the runners would hang out. Two days before the race, I brought two large duffel bags of Grandma's Marathon long sleeve shirts with me to the commons and shouted, "I have free T-shirts if you want one!" There was a long line and, in return, I received phone numbers and addresses, which I used for recruiting top-notch women athletes to Grandma's Marathon.

This was the beginning of a Grandma's Marathon tradition of developing close relationships with top U.S. elite women runners. Since 1987, Grandma's has hosted seven National Women's Championships.

One runner was Janice Ettle, the first Minnesota finisher in Olympia, placing sixth in 2:33:41. I would describe Janice as not having the purest running style, but I've rarely witnessed a male or female who raced with so much determination and guts.

Janice won Grandma's Marathon in 1982 and 1991. She was inducted into the Grandma's Marathon Hall of Fame in 2001. Janice ran five Women's Olympic Marathon Trials – 1984, 1988, 1992, 1996 and 2000. She also competed in the 10,000 meters on the track at the 1992 Olympic Trials.

In 2003, Janice ran her last competitive race – the Garry Bjorklund Half Marathon. She will always be a friend. She was a pioneer in the sport and certainly helped open the door for many women runners to achieve their goals.

Janice Ettle of St. Cloud, Minnesota receives medical attention after her 1982 first place finish at Grandma's Marathon (2:40:20).

* * *

On August 5, 1984, in Los Angeles, California, Joan Benoit won the gold medal in the first women's marathon held at the Summer Olympic Games. Joan's time was 2:24:52.

Joan had attended Grandma's Marathon numerous times as one of our guest speakers. In 2009, at the age of 52, she ran the Garry Bjorklund Half Marathon and finished in 1:20:36, still a course record for that age group.

It was always exciting to bring Joan Benoit to Duluth and have a gold medalist be part of the marathon weekend activities. She is an extraordinary person who has given much to the sport. It is a tremendous honor to know her and call her a friend.

* * *

The next leg of our western adventure was the one we had all been waiting for since setting out from Duluth. It was a four-hour drive down Highway 5 from Olympia to Eugene, Oregon. We were clueless about how we would meet Pre; we didn't even know if he was in town. There were a lot of unknowns, but as usual we figured it out on the fly. We were taking a leap of faith, but deep down in my heart I knew it would work out for us.

Upon our arrival in Eugene, we drove around attempting to get the lay of the land. We pulled over at an outdoor phone booth to see if Steve was listed in the phone book.

I had just found Pre's listing when Marty began yelling with excitement that Pre had just run by. I missed my first chance to see Pre and wasn't going to let it happen again. I ripped the page out of the phone book and took it with me.

After getting a feel for how to maneuver around Eugene, we stopped at a nearby gas station to ask directions to 4501 Franklin Boulevard. Eventually we found his trailer near the Williamette River. There was a pair of red Nike running shoes on the worn wooden steps.

We parked 50 feet from his trailer, overlooking the steep banks of the river. I excitedly got out of the camper and knocked on his door, but to my disappointment, there was no answer. We were hungry, so we decided to cook a late lunch while we waited for Pre's return. As we were cleaning our dishes, he pulled up alongside his trailer in his MG, giving us a very suspicious look.

As we approached Pre, I nervously mentioned to him that we were from Minnesota and friends with Garry Bjorklund (however, at that time, I was taking a little liberty with that statement). I explained that we were on a month-long trip out west and we wanted to stop by and say hi. I was wearing my light blue Minnesota Duluth Track t-shirt, and I think that helped Pre realize I was telling the truth.

Without hesitation, Pre responded, "Any friends of Garry Bjorklund, are friends of mine." He invited us inside his trailer. My dream of meeting my running hero was finally coming true.

We spent over two-hours with him as he shared many of his running stories. We were also introduced to Lobo, his black shepherd, whom you could tell was a very important part of Pre's life.

Pre was more than generous with his time and signed autographs and let us take pictures of him. During our visit, Steve received numerous phone calls, and his response was, "I have friends from Minnesota visiting, maybe another time." I think we were his excuse to be able to stay home and be with his dog.

We may have overstayed our welcome, but never felt it. Pre was a gracious, genuine, and giving person. We each thanked him for his kindness and wished him well with upcoming races.

Pre was a hero of mine, and by the time we left, he was also a hero of Marty and Roger.

Marty Paavola, Steve Prefontaine, and Scott Keenan at Pre's trailer in the fall of 1973.

We ended up staying in Eugene for four days and one of our visits was to Hayward Field, the track that Pre made famous. I ran four laps around it – another dream come true.

As we left town, we stopped at other phone booths and ripped out the phone book pages with Steve's name on them, souvenirs for my running friends back home. I was sad that my good friend, Ricky Brown, wasn't on the trip with us.

A special moment with Pre and his dog Lobo.

* * *

We continued to Coos Bay, Oregon, Pre's birthplace. He was born January 25, 1951. Coos Bay was a two hour drive from Eugene and I remember it being a quaint fishing community. The town was built on an S-shaped inlet where Coos River enters the Pacific Ocean, approximately ten miles away.

We took that ten-mile drive so Marty could fulfill one of his dreams of swimming in the ocean.

Afterward our trip led us to the Redwood Forest in Northern California, then on to Lake Tahoe and Carson City, Nevada, and a stopover in Reno. We were excited to go into our first casino, but I was escorted out since I wasn't 21. Marty and Roger enjoyed their evening, and I went to a movie.

Our next stop was the Salt Flats of Nevada where many world speed records have been set. We followed the endless blackline and reached 90-miles per hour.

* * *

We finally returned to Duluth after being gone 29 days. We were young and adventurous, but mostly we played it safe. I ran a total of 15 miles on the trip.

By the time we got home, I was out of money and needed to find work quickly, so I headed to the employment office in Duluth. During a brief meeting with an employment specialist, I was handed a 3 x 5-inch index card with the phone number and address of Northern Drug.

During my interview, Bob Lange, the floor manager, asked me why I'd like to work for the company. My response was simple and direct. "I just returned from a four-week trip out west and I am completely broke. If you hire me, I will work my ass off for you. I won't disappoint you." I was hired on the spot.

Years later, Bob Lange became a great friend and, in 1986, we ran every street in Duluth together – approximately 600 miles in preparation for the upcoming Grandma's Marathon.

* * *

Many months after we came back from our trip, I sent Pre a letter and a picture of him with Lobo. I once again thanked him for allowing us to visit.

On December 5, 1974, Pre wrote me a letter asking if I could send him another photo, just like the last one. He ended by mentioning that he may run some indoor races out our way.

I sent two 8 x 10-inch photos of him and Lobo. Just over six months later, on May 30, 1975, Pre died in a tragic car accident. The running world mourned.

After his death, Marty, Roger, and I went to Superior, Wisconsin, to celebrate Pre's life and reminisce about our special visit with him. As we drank cheap bar tequila, we yelled out countless times, "GO PRE!"

My friend, Marty Paavola, died on November 15, 2014, at the age of 63 from pancreatic cancer.

My friend, Roger Johnson, died on November 15, 2017, at the age of 65 from lung cancer.

I truly miss my friends.

CHAPTER 8

Paavo Nurmi Marathon

I began running again after returning from my trip and was averaging 20 to 30 miles per week. By January of 1974, I was actually training, putting in 40 to 60 miles every week. By mid-April, I upped it to 70 to 80 miles.

I didn't have the money to attend spring quarter at UMD. I needed to work and get back on my feet financially and try to save every penny I could.

I was active in our local running community as president of the North Shore Striders. It was a busy time working as many hours as I could, running more miles than ever before and managing the club.

I also focused on becoming a better runner and set two goals.

The first was to run the Paavo Nurmi Marathon in Hurley, Wisconsin on August 10, 1974. The second was to return to college in the fall and be part of the cross-country team.

The Paavo Nurmi Marathon is held annually on the second Saturday in August. The race was established in 1969 when Dr. Thomas Rosandich organized about 70 athletes from his fitness training camp to run a marathon in the northwoods of Iron County, Wisconsin. Later, the race was named for Paavo Nurmi, honoring the greatest Finnish runner of all time. He won nine Olympic gold medals.

Today, the Paavo Nurmi Marathon is the oldest marathon in Wisconsin, and the 14th oldest in the nation. The race starts in the small community of Upson and finishes on Silver Street on the main roadway in Hurley. In the mid-1970s it became one of the largest marathons in the country with 1100 participants. If you were a distance runner and from Minnesota, Wisconsin or Michigan, you needed to run Paavo.

* * *

Ricky Wilde of Cheshire, England, holds the course record at the Paavo Nurmi Marathon of 2:19:10, set in 1978. Mary Bange from La Crosse, Wisconsin set the women's course record in 1979 in 2:47:49.

I had the opportunity to meet Ricky shortly after his victory at Paavo and invited him to run Grandma's in 1979. With a lot of influence from his friend and world-class master runner, Dan Conway, of Chetek, Wisconsin, he agreed.

We had many talented runners entered in Grandma's that year, most from the Midwest. The three favorites in the men's open division were Garry Bjorklund, our hometown favorite, Barney Klecker of Chaska, Minnesota and Ricky Wilde. The race was competitive with Ricky being crowned the champion in 2:14:44. Garry finished second in 2:16:49 and Barney was one minute behind in 2:17:49.

Lorraine Moller from Auckland, New Zealand, placed 48th overall and was easily the women's champion, with a finishing time of 2:37:37. She continued her winning streak at Grandma's Marathon in 1980 and 1981. Lorraine was a rare three-time champion and her 2:29:36 in 1981 remained the course record for 19 years.

In 1992 at the Barcelona Olympics, Lorraine Moller, representing New Zealand at the age of 37, won the bronze medal in the marathon. It was stated that she ran boldly and bravely and floated to the finish line with a time of 2:33:59, only 78 seconds behind the gold medalist.

I've felt guilty all of these years that Lorraine didn't receive the proper recognition for her three victories at Grandma's.

In 1981, when Dick Beardsley ran his winning time of 2:09:37, it unfortunately overshadowed Lorraine's 2:29:36. The media was infatuated with Dick's time and the fact that he beat Garry Bjorklund.

As I look back, I wish I had played a larger role in helping Lorraine receive her due at Grandma's. I should have been much more active in promoting her.

Lorraine's 2:29:36 in 1981 ranked third in the world. Dick Beardsley's 1981, 2:09:37 ranked him tied for the fourth fastest marathon in the world. There's no mistaking that these were two of the greatest performances in Grandma's Marathon history. It helped launch us to be recognized in the world rankings.

One of the greatest running books I've ever read was *On the Wings of Mercury – the Lorraine Moller Story*. This is a book everyone should read. Lorraine is a phenomenal author.

* * *

In 1979, Grandma's Marathon surpassed the Paavo Nurmi Marathon as the largest marathon in the Upper Midwest. Kerry Louks, from Duluth, was the last person to break three hours, with a time of 2:59:58. 1134 runners out of the 1290 finishers broke four hours. Mark Wilhelmson of Duluth was the last recorded finisher with a time of 4:20:05.

* * *

In June and July of 1974, I was now averaging 80 to 100 miles each week. I participated in a number of road races leading up to my first marathon attempt.

- On June 9, I ran a 5-mile road race in a time of 27:36 (5:31 minutes per mile).
- On June 16, I finished second to my friend Scott Sundquist at the Hibbing 8-mile road race in 44:19 (5:32 minutes per mile) – very hot and hilly.

- On July 7, my second anniversary of becoming a runner, I ran the Buhl Half Marathon in 1:20:50 (6:10 minutes per mile). It was, again, hot and hilly. I finished in ninth place and was the second North Shore Striders finisher.

The following is a sample of my mileage in preparation for the 1974 Paavo Nurmi Marathon:

Monday, July 8:	5 p.m.	15 miles
Tuesday, July 9:	Noon	6 miles
	8:30 p.m.	9 miles
Wednesday, July 10	7 p.m.	13 miles
Thursday, July 11	Noon	5 miles
	7:30 p.m.	7 miles
Friday, July 12	Noon	2.5 miles
	8 p.m.	12.5 miles
Saturday, July 13	Noon	4 miles
	8:30 p.m.	9 miles
Sunday, July 14	6 p.m.	17.5 miles
Total		100.5 miles

The week of July 15 – 21, I ran 80.5 miles. On Saturday, July 20, I raced the Park Point 5-Miler and finished in 27:50. I felt sluggish and my performance was sub-par. I was tired and I had doubts that I'd be able to finish a marathon.

The week of July 22 – 28, I ran 79 miles. During that week, I did my first 20-mile run.

The week of July 29 – August 4, I ran 47.5 miles. My running log indicated that my right Achilles tendon was inflamed and sore. I took two days off.

Monday, August 5	10 miles
Tuesday, August 6	10 miles
Wednesday, August 7	8 miles
Thursday, August 8	0 miles – sore Achilles tendon
Friday, August 9	0 miles – sore Achilles tendon

Saturday was the Paavo Nurmi Marathon. I was scared. This was my biggest running challenge, and I had a sore Achilles tendon.

The evening before the race, I took the two-hour drive to Hurley and found an empty parking lot a few blocks from the center of downtown. This was the first time I had visited Hurley.

My plan was to sleep in my pick-up. Unfortunately, the parking lot I chose was near a bar. It was a poor choice. People were coming and going all night and were ear-piercingly loud. I slept no more than four hours before I boarded a yellow school bus to the starting line.

I met up with two friends and members of the North Shore Striders, Jess Koski and Pat Folman, at the starting line. Our plan was simple – run together and break three-hours. The course was run on a secluded forest roadway with many hills and turns. It was very scenic, and extremely challenging.

During the first 17 miles we were on a pace to break three hours, but it seemed so slow that I was getting impatient. Jess was an experienced runner at long distances who had run two previous marathons – a 3:16 in 1971 and a 3:05 in 1972. He warned me numerous times not to speed up because we still had a long way to go.

Of course, shortly afterward, I ignored his warnings and increased my pace, moving away from my running partners. Everything was going great, and I was on a 2:45 marathon pace until mile 21 when I developed severe stomach cramps that forced me to a crawl.

The race quickly became a nightmare, and I suffered every step. Finally, I was approaching "Cemetery Hill" with a mile to go. It was a long uphill with the town's cemetery on the right side of the road. My cramps finally brought me to a complete halt, and I began vomiting orange color bile two feet in front of me. It must have looked like a scene from the movie The Exorcist to the spectators.

Earlier in the race, I drank a sugary orange colored energy drink at each water station. The taste was wonderful, but drinking it turned out to be another rookie mistake.

Dennis McNulty of Greenwood, Indiana, age 29, pulled alongside me and asked if I was all right. I responded, "I feel great now!" Dennis suggested we finish together. We ran a fast pace and as we approached the finish line on Silver Street, he grabbed my hand, and we raised our arms together with personal victories. We tied for 42nd place with a time of 2:51:01 (6:31 per mile). Jess finished in 2:53:12 and Pat in 2:57:28.

At the finish line, participants were offered a bowl of Kalamojakka (fish head soup) to help with recovery.

I made one more mistake that day, allowing the fire department to hose me down to clean up and cool off. I almost went into shock and was beginning to go into a state of hypothermia. I walked as fast as I could back to my truck and turned the heat on.

Even though I felt I should have run faster, I did meet my goal of breaking three hours. It was a happy day.

* * *

In the two weeks after the Paavo Nurmi Marathon, I ran 28 miles. My calf muscles were extremely tight, and my right Achilles tendon was again inflamed. My body wasn't recovering well.

I did return to UMD during fall quarter and joined the cross-country team as well. I finished my first collegiate 5-mile race on October 5, 1974 in 27:18.

My race times became slower and slower each week. I was tired all the time and wasn't reacting well to coach Rynda's workouts. I also developed a bad cold with swollen glands. To be honest, I couldn't wait for the season to be over.

CHAPTER 9

The Summer of '75

I averaged 50 miles per week from January 1 – June 1, 1975. I was continuing my education at UMD but didn't join the track team. I wasn't enjoying my experiences running at the collegiate level. It was time for a break.

I was injury free during this time, only suffering from a few winter colds.

In June and July, I increased my mileage to 75 miles per week and quickly improved my overall fitness level. On July 5, I ran in the United States AAU Senior 25-Kilometer National Championships in Buhl, Minnesota. Jim Randall, an attorney from Hibbing, was the race director and a member of the North Shore Striders. Jim was a good runner and a fantastic race director.

Buhl is 75 miles northwest of Duluth and 12 miles north of Hibbing on Highway 169. It is literally in the middle of nowhere.

Minnesota Distance Running Association members, Jeff Brain and Pat Lanin, were mainly responsible for lobbying for the national championship race.

Word spread to elite runners throughout the United States that there was a national championship race in northern Minnesota.

In September of 1985, David Kayser wrote an article for *Running Times Magazine*, titled "The Summer of 75". He recapped the essence of why runners would take a journey to run in a small town that few people have heard of. Buhl is less than 100 miles from the Canadian border surrounded by bogs, small crystal clear lakes and the unofficial Minnesota state bird – the mosquito.

Some of the best runners in the United States packed their cars and traveled to the Midwest for the race on the Fourth of July weekend. Runners came from Washington DC, Vermont, Missouri, California, Wisconsin, and Minnesota.

Randall had a budget of $1,020 to cover all event expenses, which included a few dollars for gas money for some of the elite.

Back then, runners ran for the pure love of the sport and to compete. There was no prize money. It was always an honor to race against the best and everyone was thankful for the race directors' and volunteers' hard work.

Jim Randall was an all-time great host as he fed dozens of runners and allowed everyone to crash at his home. None of us had money to spend on hotel rooms.

The race started at Lake Leander on an asphalt highway, with a broad gravel shoulder. It was described on the entry form as being held in the northwoods on a rolling course with almost no traffic. The entry fee was $2.

Steve Hoag from Anoka, Minnesota, and a member of the Twin Cities Track Club, was the favorite. In April, Steve finished second at the Boston Marathon in 2:11:54, the fourth-fastest time in the world that year. Bill Rodgers won in 2:09. Just over two months later, Steve won the 25K National Championships in Buhl with a time of 1:23:24. Bob Fitts from the Saint Louis Track Club was second in 1:24:02.

Roger Pekuri from Ironwood, Michigan, was the first North Shore Strider to finish, placing 18th in 1:31:09. Al Zetterlund was the second Strider in 27th place in 1:34:20. I was the third Strider, in 29th place (1:34:55). My pace was 6:38 per mile. It was a good race for me.

David Kayser, the author of the "Summer of 75," finished 17th (1:30:41).

In February of 1984, Governor Rudy Perpich appointed Jim Randall to become a judge with the Minnesota Court of Appeals. Jim served in this role until his retirement in 2008.

Perpich, also from Hibbing, became Minnesota's Governor in 1982, and served two four-year terms. In the mid-1980's Governor Perpich saved Grandma's Marathon from extinction. In

2006, the race honored his great work by naming a public service award after him.

Steve Hoag passed away on September 15, 2017, at the age of 70 from complications from a lung transplant. The running world remembered his life at his funeral in Anoka.

* * *

On June 14, 1975, just three weeks before the 25K National Championships, a group of North Shore Striders traveled to Macalester College in Saint Paul, Minnesota, to participate in the Minnesota AAU track championships. The races were $1 each. I ran the 3-mile at 9:20 a.m. and finished in 15:25 (5:08 per mile). At 9:20 p.m., under the lights on the track, I ran a 32:09 six mile, which I averaged 5:21 per mile.

We all finished in the middle of the pack among many of Minnesota's best runners participating in the meet. It didn't matter though. We were competing as a team and were proud to be wearing our North Shore Striders colors.

I just completed my third year as a runner, and noted in my training log, "IT IS TIME TO TRAIN!"

Later in the fall, on November 8, a number of UMD runners and North Shore Striders decided to enter in the AAU Cross Country Championships held at Lake Nokomis in Minneapolis. It was a nice, but breezy day and I met my goal of breaking 32 minutes, finishing in 31:56. If memory serves me, that put me in 22nd place. My mile splits were: 4:58, 5:16, 5:26, 5:24, 5:34 and 5:18.

In the spring of 1976, I reluctantly returned, under peer pressure, to the UMD track team. In the month of March, I only ran 28 miles because of a severe case of bronchitis. I was really sick.

My first race of the track season was a 15:43 three-mile event. I felt horrible, tired and out of shape. Five days later, coach

Rynda signed me up to compete in the 6-mile (24 laps) in River Falls, Wisconsin. Somehow the running gods were with me that day, running the race of my life. It made no sense, but I finished in 31:07.9 (5:11 per mile). I shocked myself, my teammates and coach Rynda.

Mile 1 – 5:00 minutes
Mile 2 – 5:09 minutes
Mile 3 – 5:15 minutes
Mile 4 – 5:15 minutes
Mile 5 – 5:19 minutes
Mile 6 – 5:09 minutes

As I look back, I was probably well rested for the first time in my racing life. This was an important lesson and I applied it to my 14 years as a college and high school cross country coach.

CHAPTER 10

We're Off and Running

1977 Grandma's Marathon Poster.

On Sunday, August 29, 1976, Bob Schneider organized the inaugural Billings Park 10K Road Race in Superior, Wisconsin. The course was described as out and back with rolling hills through residential and wooded portions of the park. The roadway was 50 percent pavement and 50 percent dirt. The entry fee was 50 cents.

The North Shore Striders hosted their annual club meeting afterward in the picnic area overlooking a scenic inlet of the Saint Louis River.

There were a dozen or so Striders at the meeting to discuss a plan to organize a United States sanctioned marathon along the shores of Lake Superior on Scenic Highway 61. This was the only agenda item. The starting line would be just outside of Two Harbors and the race would finish in the industrial waterfront area now known as Canal Park.

This was the largest endeavor the club had ever taken on and I needed consensus from the most active members. The date that would best fit our busy summer race schedule was June 25, 1977. I had confidence we could put together a quality race since we had been hosting an annual Muscular Dystrophy 26-Mile Run-a-Thon since 1975 on the first Saturday of August. The course would be almost identical.

After enjoying a post-race celebration and a little discussion, club members voted unanimously to support hosting a marathon in late June. The North Shore Striders had $23.50 in the club's checkbook.

I would be the race director and my first responsibility was to put the finances together. Our other races were always on a shoestring budget. We just needed the bare essentials, nothing fancy – road racing was still in its infancy. Runners had low expectations, they just wanted an accurately measured course and to not get hit by a car.

We had less than ten months to pull this together. I needed a budget, to finalize the racecourse, find a major sponsor, market the race and find a team of volunteers. It was a lot of work for a short amount of time. I was ready for the challenge but, to be honest, I was scared.

It was an ideal time to start a marathon, as the running boom in the United States was taking off. Many give credit for the boom to the success of Frank Shorter winning Olympic gold in the marathon in Munich in 1972.

Marathons were popping up in cities across the country including Seattle, New York, Portland, Honolulu and Cleveland.

Jim Fixx released his best-selling book, *The Complete Book of Running,* in 1977, about the same time that Grandma's Marathon was sending 150 runners down Old Scenic Highway 61. Jim is also credited with helping to start America's fitness revolution by extolling the health benefits of regular jogging.

My desire to start a marathon was certainly influenced by running the 1974 Paavo Nurmi Marathon and by entering the United States AAU 25K National Championships in Buhl. We also knew we had one of the most beautiful and scenic racecourses in our own backyard, and it was a fast route.

I began organizing North Shore Strider races in 1973. I truly enjoyed it and my goal was always to organize a good and safe race but, most importantly, I wanted to make it a fun race. I actually enjoyed it much more than running the races. I was able to express myself in a different way and, for good or bad, I liked being in charge.

In 1977, I was the race director for the following races:

- Smelt Run 6-Mile – April 30
- Spirit Mountain 10-Mile – May 14
- Skyline Parkway 5-Mile – June 4
- Minnesota AAU 15K Championship – June 18
- Grandma's Marathon – June 25
- Greek-a-thon 10K – July 10
- Park Point 5-Miler – July 16

It was a busy spring and summer with one race after another. Now we added a major event to our schedule – a marathon. With a $649.51 budget in hand, I approached high profile local businesses, attempting to convince them to sponsor our marathon. We had no business plan and no marketing plan. Everything would be based on trust. I was rejected each time.

People who know me, most would agree that I'm a little headstrong and stubborn. I don't give up easily. I scheduled a meeting with Mick Paulucci and Andy Borg at the properties of their newly opened Grandma's Saloon and Deli, which is a stone's throw from the Aerial Lift Bridge. It was right where we wanted to finish the race.

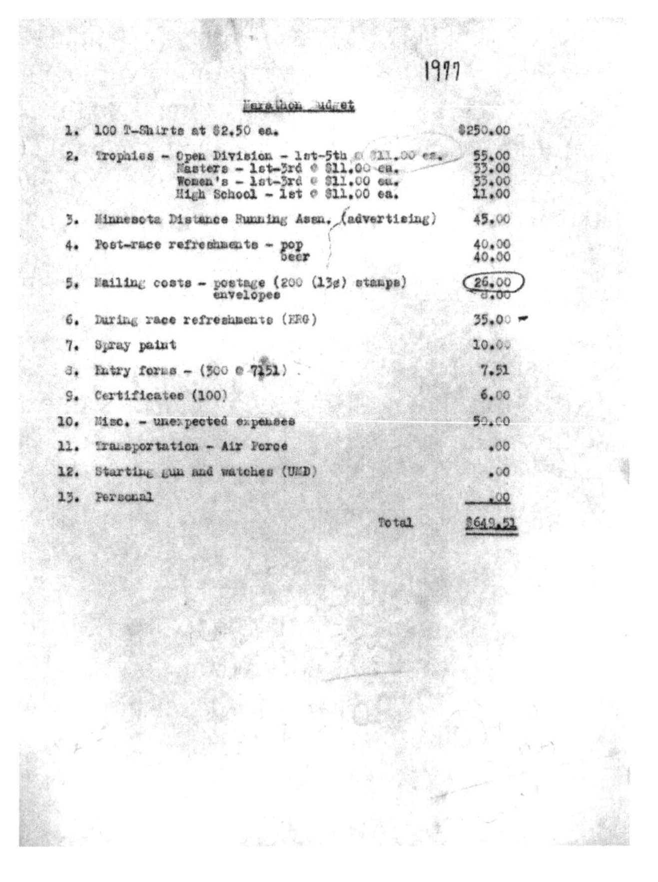

1977

Marathon Budget

1.	100 T-Shirts at $2.50 ea.	$250.00
2.	Trophies - Open Division - 1st-5th @ $11.00 ea.	55.00
	Masters - 1st-3rd @ $11.00 ea.	33.00
	Women's - 1st-3rd @ $11.00 ea.	33.00
	High School - 1st @ $11.00 ea.	11.00
3.	Minnesota Distance Running Assn. (advertising)	45.00
4.	Post-race refreshments - pop	40.00
	beer	40.00
5.	Mailing costs - postage (200 (13¢) stamps)	26.00
	envelopes	8.00
6.	During race refreshments (ERG)	35.00
7.	Spray paint	10.00
8.	Entry forms - (300 @ 7151)	7.51
9.	Certificates (100)	6.00
10.	Misc. - unexpected expenses	50.00
11.	Transportation - Air Force	.00
12.	Starting gun and watches (UMD)	.00
13.	Personal	.00
	Total	$649.51

$649.51 was the North Shore Strider's budget for the inaugural Grandma's Marathon in 1977.

My strategy changed slightly for this meeting. I had just turned 23 and was skinny, fast-talking, and gaunt looking. I felt it was important to bring a fellow strider with me – a more professional approach was needed. George Fink, a 37-year-old sales manager at Northwestern Bell, fit the bill. George was a member of the University of Minnesota Track and Field team in 1956 and 1957. He had a warm personality and a smile that made you want to be his friend.

I would have done almost anything to get this deal finalized even if it meant giving a title sponsorship away for $600. George and I made the deal that beautiful September afternoon. We received our asking price and agreed to finish almost at the back door of the saloon. There was no signed agreement, no contract, only the four of us shaking hands.

I can't thank Mick and Andy enough for trusting us and playing a major role in getting the marathon started. As we grew, they never flinched once and have always been there helping us become a world-class race with small-town charm.

George Fink, Mick Paulucci and Andy Borg were inducted into the inaugural Grandma's Marathon Hall of Fame Class in 1996. George died on September 10, 2012. He was 73. Mick died on August 8, 2020, at 71.

* * *

John Leppi, 44, was one of the senior members of our club. He had a PhD in anatomy from Yale University and was one of the founding faculty at UMD's Medical School. He was chairman of the school's department of Biomedical Anatomy for 19 years.

John was instrumental in starting Grandma's Marathon. He was an active runner who often won the master's division in our local races. He was professional in everything he did. He was the perfect person to measure the racecourse. John did the research on how to do it correctly and purchased a Jones Counter, a device fitted to the front of the wheel of a bicycle to count the revolutions. It was invented by Alan Jones in 1971, specifically to measure the length of road racecourses.

John, with support from his son, Peter, measured and finalized the course twice for accuracy. This was a huge relief. We had our course.

John Leppi finished 45th that first year, with a time of 3:26:21 on the course he measured. He was the fourth finisher over 40 years old. John died on May 12, 2010, in Honolulu, Hawaii.

* * *

Brian Larsen was born in 1956, in Grand Marias, Minnesota, which has now become a hotbed for summer tourism. Grand Marais is the gateway to the Boundary Waters up the narrow and undulating Gunflint Trail. This national treasure has over 1.1 million acres of interconnecting lakes and rivers, surrounded by the unspoiled Superior National Forest.

Grand Marais, population of 1,300, is well-known for quaint bistros and spring-like cool temperatures that give a welcome relief from the hot summer days for Minnesota tourists.

Brian Larsen was a talented but unknown runner who escaped death twice – from a tragic car accident and a logging mishap.

On August 11, 1973, at the Paavo Nurmi Marathon, Brian, wearing a dark blue fish net singlet, white cotton shorts and calf high tube socks, ran 2:34:59. He had just turned 17 and, without knowing it, ran the fifth fastest marathon in the country for his age. On almost any other course and with cooler temperatures, Brian would have easily run a sub-2:30 that day.

Brian beat many experienced and accomplished Minnesota runners at Paavo including Scott Sundquist, Jeff Brain, John Cramer, Bruce Mortenson and Dennis Fee. Dennis was from White Bear Lake, and a year earlier, in 1972, crushed the Minnesota High

School 2-Mile state record by more than 15 seconds. His time of 8:59.3 was a record that stood until 2000. Dennis Fee is recognized as one of the all-time top 10 Minnesota Distance Runners.

Brian beat Dennis that hot August day in Hurley, Wisconsin by exactly four minutes.

Brian and I were college roommates in 1977. This was also the year I joined the running store business with a dentist from Babbitt, Minnesota. We leased a 400 square foot office space in the Kenwood Shopping Center. Shoes were stacked to the ceiling, and on any spare space I hung photos of Steve Prefontaine from my trip out west.

We were the first exclusive running store in Duluth, and I named it The Running Shop. Brian worked in the store for $5 an hour.

I quit the business one year later and soon after I found myself in a lawsuit. My partner accused me of stealing inventory. This was a very difficult and busy time for me and now I was being accused of a crime.

I won the lawsuit but ended up paying thousands of dollars for accounting and attorney's fees. In many ways, I felt I earned a degree in business with this challenging experience.

In early June 1977, my dad donated 50 gallons of old multi-colored paint to the race. After mixing everything together in a large metal drum we were left with a puke brown color.

Brian and I were on a mission to paint one square block of an old rusty, dilapidated, corrugated sheet metal fence that surrounded a century- old scrap yard near the finish line. There were tons of junk cars and metal scrap, with old batteries and dangerous wires sticking out of the soiled ground.

Our intent was to spruce up the finish area for the runners as they approached the final straightaway. The area was dirty and had an old industrial look, but at least there would be a fresh coat of paint on the ugly fence.

Our reward after painting was a free burger and fries at Grandma's Saloon & Deli

Brian Larsen and Ricky Brown were with me on race day as we followed Garry Bjorklund along the racecourse at the first Grandma's Marathon. I was driving a blue metallic Chevy Nova hatchback and as Brian recalls, I was concerned about the possibility of getting a flat tire with my well-worn $5 tires.

We were the timing crew.

Brian continues to volunteer for the marathon each year. His unselfishness and love for the race landed him in our Hall of Fame in 2001. He was an unknown runner and an unknown volunteer who has made a huge difference in the start and development of Grandma's Marathon.

2001 Grandma's Marathon hall of Fame Inductees. Front: Paul Van Winkel. Back: Brian Daugherty, Brian Larsen, and Janice Ettle.

* * *

I will never forget driving down the dusty dead-end dirt road, a few blocks north of the last commercial business in Two

Harbors. I was on my way to visit Dr. Gerald "Jerry" Church for our initial planning meeting.

It was in early spring of 1977 and Jerry, a North Shore Striders member, was in charge of setting up the starting area for Grandma's Marathon.

His family home is on the shores of Burlington Bay, a scenic setting on Lake Superior. It could be best described as harmonious and tranquil. It overlooked the crystal blue waters of Gitche Gumee. The shoreline is surrounded by towering white pines and the chatter of countless birds. Loons and ducks are often found nesting in the nearby secluded estuary.

I always looked forward to these meetings for 20 straight years. I needed to schedule at least three hours of time.

Jerry was a detail person. He carried a small pocket-sized notebook with an equal size pencil in his short sleeve shirt pocket. Our meetings usually began with a light lunch, followed by a stroll along the outer banks of his property.

You could see it in his eyes and hear it in his voice how proud he was of raising eight wonderful children in his paradise. Jerry's wife, Joanne, with her wavy red hair was the backbone behind raising the children - Ivy, Jennifer, Lili, Holly, Lon, Amy, Andrew, and David.

Jerry was lean and of modest height. You could easily guess he was a runner. Jerry was 50 when we had our first meeting in 1977. He was a family physician who delivered generations of babies and was described by many of his patients as gentle, caring and passionate.

There was a small green cabin adjacent to the house where Jerry stored many of his marathon supplies. The larger homemade signs, posts and banners were kept in an older blue shed with a lean-to structure attached. Everything was itemized and inventoried.

The starting line was no more than 200 feet from where the expressway intersects with the scenic highway just outside of Two Harbors. Lon, a middle child and the oldest son, was recruited by his father to assist on race day. One of their jobs was to construct the biffies, which back then were a colony of several 2 x 4 wooden benches that were set up in the adjoining woods with toilet paper rolls dangling off nearby tree branches. A large, slightly worn grey canvas separated the men from the women, and small hand painted signs gave directions.

On the morning of the first Grandma's Marathon, the starting gun fired at exactly 11 a.m. and 150 runners, mostly from Minnesota, were on their way to Duluth on a hot summer day.

Lon Church was the lead bicycle rider, equipped with a red fluorescent flag with a wooden stick attached. He painted a small sign that read "Marathon In Progress" and taped it to the front of his 10-speed bike. Lon was planning to ride the first seven miles to Knife River, but clearly saw the need to lead Garry Bjorklund all the way to the finish line. The course was only modestly closed, meaning there was much traffic to be moved aside.

Jerry Church, after a quick cleanup at the start, began his journey to Duluth and finished 82nd with a time of 4:02:29. There were 116 finishers that day.

Jerry continued his role as starting line director for 20 years. He died on February 24, 1997, from melanoma. He was the sole inductee into the Grandma's Marathon Hall of Fame that year.

Jerry's wife, Joanne, still lives in the family home at age 90. The blue shed was recently torn down due to age.

* * *

Dorothy Spencer, her husband, Roger, and their two children, Brad and Sherri, moved to Duluth in June of 1975. They purchased a secluded family home on Columbus Avenue where they'd reside for the next four and a half years.

Dorothy is a high-energy person, with a diminutive body and is gifted with a high degree of organizational skills. She soon became the administrative assistant for Greg Fox, vice chancellor at UMD.

Roger was much more laid back with his easy going and relaxing personality, the direct opposite of Dorothy. He accepted a manager position at Goldfine's by the Bridge, one of the nation's first discount stores.

Dorothy and Roger were active runners, and it was only natural to become North Shore Striders.

If I could have a second mother, it would have been Dorothy. She was always gracious in sharing her time and home in the early years of planning Grandma's Marathon. Her lower-level family room ended up as our race headquarters. The floor was covered with runner packets and race supplies. Roger smiled and seemed not to care that his home was taken over.

Dorothy often volunteered at our club races and was quickly becoming a mainstay with the North Shore Striders. We counted on her for almost everything.

Dorothy and I shared the same vision in getting Grandma's Marathon started. She would be in charge of recording results at the finish line for the first four years. I felt a sense of calm with her there, especially when I began to get frazzled.

* * *

Dorothy, of Chinese heritage, is adventurous and once spent six weeks by herself biking through China. One of her rides was from Shanghai to Beijing, over 800 miles. She enjoyed stopping at villages, visiting and giving small gifts to the people in the local communities.

Mount Everest is the world's tallest peak at 29,029 feet and straddles the boarder of China and Nepal. This would be another exploration for Dorothy. She hired a Sherpa to guide her to the camp at 19,600 feet, for a challenge that many of us would find impossible.

In 1977, I ran many times with Roger in his preparation for Grandma's Marathon. One of our runs, of longer length, was on gravel back roads that ran between two older cemeteries. Roger finished his first marathon at Grandma's in 99th place in 4:34:47.

The Spencers moved to Minnetonka, Minnesota in late fall of 1979. Roger died shortly afterward on November 16, 1980, of a heart infection. Dorothy's life was turned upside down and she struggled for many years with her loss.

The one constant in life was her annual trek to Duluth to volunteer at Grandma's Marathon. She brought a half-dozen race clocks from event organizations in the Minneapolis area to be used on the racecourse for timing. She always arrived on Wednesday afternoon of race week. Her duties included running errands, answering phones and planning the award ceremony.

On race morning, Dorothy worked the finish line, which she painted the afternoon before.

For 40 years, Dorothy was a godsend to Grandma's Marathon. She loved coming home to northern Minnesota and having a reunion with so many of her friends. It was an important part of her life.

Dorothy now lives and enjoys life in a beautiful lake home not far from Tomahawk, Wisconsin. She has found peace and happiness as she lives each day to the fullest.

Dorothy has run Grandma's Marathon twice and completed ten marathons. She was inducted into the inaugural class of the Grandma's Marathon Hall of Fame in 1996.

1996 Hall of Fame Inductees, left to right: John Foschi, Garry Bjorklund, Andy Borg, Dorothy Spencer, Mick Paulucci, George Fink, and Alex Rattelle, M.D.

* * *

My Air National Guard meetings were scheduled for the last weekend each month. I was a firefighter in the Civil Engineer "Prime Beef" unit. Our main responsibilities were to build runways wherever needed in the world.

We had our tropic and arctic bags packed and stored. We were always on a 24-hour notice to fly out.

During my March drill weekend in 1977, I put in a request with my captain to get Saturday, June 25 and Sunday, June 26 off. The standard practice was to make up the drill within the next two weeks. I explained I was the race director for a new marathon from Two Harbors to Duluth. My request was rejected, and my captain further proclaimed that I would be considered AWOL if I didn't show up.

I didn't know what to do, but I had to do something. I decided to go over his head, and made an appointment with Colonel Wayne Gatlin, the commander of the base. My haircut was shorter than regulation for the meeting.

Colonel Gatlin acknowledged that he liked runners and would arrange for me to make up the drill. I expressed my gratitude and thanked him numerous times.

In 1980, Wayne Gatlin became a major general. When opportunities arise, I continue to give him credit for saving Grandma's Marathon.

I once attended a social gathering, which General Gatlin and his family were attending, and I shared my story about our meeting in 1977. They were all pleased to hear it and were full of smiles.

I received my honorable discharge on December 1, 1977, only five months after the inaugural Grandma's Marathon. It was a difficult five months as my captain wasn't happy with me for going over his head.

General Gatlin died on January 16, 2012, at the age of 91.

* * *

In 2016, Shane Bauer, the executive director of Grandma's Marathon, honored me by creating an annual award in my name. I was excited and grateful for the recognition but had one stipulation. I would need to select the annual recipient.

I've put a great deal of pressure on myself in choosing the most deserving person. I want to pick someone who has truly represented Grandma's Marathon at the highest level.

My criteria includes how people have endured me over the years, especially during the most challenging moments in which I may have been a little brash. I look for individuals who have played a major factor in the development and growth of our events. I look for people who understood my goal of building a life-long community event that would be cherished and loved for future generations.

In 1977, another unknown runner, Wendy Hovland, 18, from Hoyt Lakes, Minnesota, entered Grandma's Marathon.

Wendy was my clear choice to receive the 2019 Scott Keenan Founder Award. Here is my introduction of Wendy to the crowd at the sponsorship celebration banquet the evening of the race:

This is a great day for Grandma's Marathon and myself, as I have the pleasure to introduce a special individual who has made a tremendous contribution to women's running in Minnesota, the Upper Midwest and the nation.

Grandma's Marathon began on Saturday, June 25, 1977, with 150 registered runners and 116 finishers. The entry was $3, which included a bus ride to the starting line, a red finisher t-shirt and, of course, a free beer after the race.

The temperature was extremely warm, reaching in the mid-80's – full sun and not a cloud in the sky. I think we all would consider this brutal running conditions. It was a black flag day before there was such a thing.

Of the 150 runners there were around 15 women registered participants, not many women, but we had the best runners from Minneapolis in the race. Susan Cushman, Alexandra Boies, who is now in the Minnesota Track and Field Hall of Fame, and Cheryl Westrum, who eventually became our 1978 champion. And, of course, we had our hometown hero, Garry Bjorklund, in the race.

History is very important to all of us and on June 25, 1977, not one of the Minneapolis women elite was crowned champion. It was Wendy Hovland from Hoyt Lakes, an 18-year-old Iron Ranger who just completed her freshman year at the University of Wisconsin Eau Claire. Wendy was a young runner, but she definitely did her homework on the roads before she made the voyage to Duluth. Wendy ran a wonderful race in a time of 3:23:39. To this day it was her first and only marathon.

In 1972, Congress voted in the Title IX Act that says "No person in the United States shall on the basis of sex be excluded from participation in, be denied the benefits of or be subjected to discrimination."

Also, in 1972, the Boston Marathon finally sanctioned women to participate in their race.

In 1977, across our country women's running and athletics in general were still in their infancy. Wendy's accomplishment on that hot June day in 1977 was really a big deal. Wendy led the way as a pioneer in this great sport. She paved the way for many other women to find the courage to say, "Yes! I can compete with not just women, but men too."

Yes, Wendy was a true pioneer with tremendous courage. She was determined to compete in a marathon when others questioned if she could. She took the challenge straight on with a full steam ahead approach.

Wendy was competitive and she ran with pure determination, she was tough, persistent and maybe a little crazy, but for sure she was a pioneer that helped put Grandma's Marathon on the map.

Wendy Hovland-Craig is a true hero of Grandma's Marathon and I am honored to award her the 2019 Scott A. Keenan Founder's Award.

My wife, Carrie, and I invited Wendy and her family to our traditional Sunday afternoon post-race barbeque. It's actually a party with great food, wine, and a little story telling. We also take it as an opportunity to share our backyard gardens with others. Everyone chips in with the grilling.

This was the first time since 1977 that Wendy and I had seen each other. She and her husband, Casey, have now become dear friends of ours.

Wendy Hovland, 18, from Hoyt Lakes, Minnesota, celebrates her 1977 Grandma's Marathon victory (3:23:39).

CHAPTER 11

Pates – Everything is Off the Record

A tennis player, a novice runner and a 1973 graduate of the University of St. Thomas in St. Paul, Minnesota, Kevin Pates had just received his bachelor's degree in journalism. He worked the next two years at the University of Illinois, and then accepted a writing gig for the Fan Newspaper of the Chicago Bears.

Pates always had a desire to work for a daily newspaper and, with an inside scoop from a friend, learned of a job opening at the Duluth News Tribune. The interview went well, and he was on his way to a career as a sportswriter that spanned more than 35 years.

Pates, with a slight stature, stood tall with his professional academic mien. At times, I could sense a cynical tone that brought a smile or maybe a little laughter to my day.

Pates began his new position in April of 1978. His first major responsibility was to cover the second annual Grandma's Marathon on June 24. The race was growing and deserved attention from the local paper.

There were 667 registered runners from 15 states. Canada was the lone foreign country represented. It was a cool morning along the shores of Lake Superior, with a 9 a.m. starting temperature of 58 degrees and overcast.

Kevin Pates, Duluth News Tribune, right, chats with Gene Niemi after the 1985 Grandma's.

Mike Slack of St. Paul and Barney Klecker of Long Prairie, Minnesota, were the favorites. Pates was looking for the inside stories from the runners' perspective. He hopped on a yellow school bus departing from Grandma's Saloon & Deli's parking lot shortly before 8 a.m.

Pates wanted to feel what the runners were feeling, find out about their training, their running background and where they were from. He had a story to write for the Sunday morning paper.

In his article, Pates wrote, "Keenan kept the brightly clad mob informed – one minute to the start!"

I was once again driving my blue Chevrolet Nova hatchback. Pates joined me for the ride down Highway 61 as part of the timing team.

We cautiously drove down the course, passing Lloyd's Bait Shop & Tackle, the Clifton Fire Department and the Lake Breeze Motel at Mile 16. We stopped at all water stations and checkpoints. Mike Slack was holding a healthy lead over Barney Klecker as the race was developing.

At mile 23, near Lemon Drop Restaurant, Slack was feeling fatigued and running on empty. He finally surrendered to the day and dropped out from exhaustion at Eighth Avenue East, near mile 25.

Klecker, 27, won the race with an awe-inspiring finish, with a course record of 2:18:42, beating Kerry Mayer of Milwaukee, Wisconsin, by almost five minutes. Klecker was a 1973 University of Wisconsin-Stout graduate and was heading back to Menomonie, Wisconsin, working on his master's degree in vocational administration. Klecker finished second to Garry Bjorklund in the inaugural Grandma's in 1977.

There were other impressive races that day, including that of a 53-year-old anesthesiologist from Edina, Minnesota. Pates wrote that Dr. Alex Ratelle beamed as he scanned the finish chart. Alex was in eighth place overall with a time of 2:31:56, and in the process set a national record for his age group.

Alex went on to finish 21 straight years at Grandma's Marathon through 1997. He once held eight world age group records and 32 American age group bests. Alex was inducted into the inaugural Grandma's Marathon Hall of Fame Class in 1996.

Alex's life included 60 missions as a navigator in a B-17 bomber with the Army Air Corps during World War II. He was shot down twice, but only sustained minor injuries.

A native of International Falls, Minnesota, Alex died in his retirement home in Grand Marais on June 10, 2012. He was 87.

116 runners finished the inaugural Grandma's Marathon, including Alex Ratelle, then 52, who came in fourth with a time of 2:37:32.

David House, 18, was our Canadian representative, recently graduating from high school in Thunder Bay, Ontario. Pates wrote, "House fell to the ground nearly unconscious 15 yards short of the finish line. He managed to pick himself up, cross the line and then collapsed again." Pates described that oxygen and care from attendant, Don Roach, brought House around.

Pates quoted House later in the day saying, "This was my first marathon and I felt good until 20 miles." His ninth-place finish – 2:32:05 – got him a plaque at the award ceremony. House's time that day in 1978 is still a Grandma's Marathon course record for runners 18 and under. It is an amazing record of longevity, matched by no other entrant.

Cheryl Westrum of Bloomington, Minnesota, was the women's champion. The 24-year-old placed 104th overall in 2:57:14 – a large improvement over her time a year earlier when finishing sixth for the women in 3:39:19.

As the years went on, I developed a love/hate relationship with the media. There were times when media members were looking for a controversial story.

In 2006, I disqualified the women's winner, 37-year-old Halina Karnatsevich of Belarus, following confirmation from USA Track and Field that she tested positive for the prohibited substance, Stanozolol, an anabolic steroid. She forfeited her $8,000 prize money and runner-up Svetlana Nekhorosh, 32, of Ukraine was named the Grandma's women's winner. Karnatsevich was banned from all competition for two years.

I was quoted after being interviewed as saying, "Let's catch the cheats. We want a clean sport! We want a level playing field for everyone."

When we sent out a press release regarding the disqualification, numerous members of the local and state media were insisting this had created a black eye for Grandma's Marathon. I refused to agree with the narrative. I insisted, with full confidence, that we caught a cheat and were doing our job in a responsible way to ensure a clean sport.

In the early 1980s, Steve Greenfield was the first media director for Grandma's Marathon. He was also the public relations director for Grandma's Restaurant Corporate office. From that time on, to my retirement, I always had a media director for the race.

I remember when my friend, Marty Paavola, once said to me, "I thought you were in charge of the race, but I keep hearing this other guy (Greenfield) on the radio." I explained, "Isn't it great? I can be the director and I don't have to talk to the media."

The truth was that I never felt comfortable on camera or with a microphone in my face. I hated watching the news afterwards and seeing my interview. I also disliked the times when they asked dumb questions.

Although on important issues that arose over the years, when members of the media really wanted to talk to me, I was always there with a smile on my face, answering their questions. I knew in my heart that the media was an extremely important part of our growth. In 2000, I started our annual luncheon to honor a member of the media for their service in covering Grandma's Marathon. It was named after "Mr. Sports of the Twin Ports" –

Marsh Nelson, a television and radio personality in Duluth for nearly 40 years.

Pates was the first recipient of this award. In 2010, Pates was also inducted into the Grandma's Marathon Hall of Fame and to this day he remains the lone media member given this honor.

One of the highlights for Pates each year was having the opportunity to meet and interview elite runners from all over the world.

My dream early on for the evolution of Grandma's Marathon was to invite runners from different nations across the globe to be a part of our event. I wanted to showcase our race and our city to the world. My dream each year was to have our own Olympics and bring in as many international runners as possible to be a part of it. We often had runners from all 50 states, but that simply wasn't good enough for me.

Here is a list of most of the countries that had runners compete in Duluth in early summer: Tanzania, Switzerland, Japan, Sri Lanka, Costa Rica, Ethiopia, Moldova, Tunisia, Italy, Norway, Poland, Kyrgyzstan, Zimbabwe, St. Lucia, Belgium, Brazil, Sweden, Scotland, China, Spain, South Africa, Canada, Ukraine, Peru, Portugal, Burundi, Puerto Rico, Morocco, Bermuda, Australia, England, Mexico, New Zealand, Belarus, Cuba, South Korea, Russia, Kenya, Zambia, Ecuador, Uganda, Hungary, Venezuela and Ireland.

In 1993, I believe for the first time in the history of the United States, Cuba was allowed to send a national team to participate in a U.S. marathon, and Grandma's Marathon was chosen.

Over the years, I received some negative feedback from other elite runners, many I consider friends, questioning the logic of bringing foreign athletes to Grandma's. I never understood their views. I didn't listen to them as I was steadfast in having Grandma's Marathon, in a small way, help enrich our cultural understanding of countries throughout the world.

My relationship with Pates for those 35 years was extremely strong, but professional. I always knew that Grandma's

Marathon would receive a fair and accurate account from his writings.

When I decided to retire in early May of 2013, Pates would be the one to tell my story to the stakeholders of the marathon. I got scolded from a few of our board members who wanted to have a controlled media release that they would sign off on. They didn't feel comfortable having it done my way.

Pates wrote the story, and he did it well. We both retired from our professions in 2013. It seemed to be the appropriate way.

Pates now lives in Sun City, Arizona, and loves the heat of the desert. In 1981, at Grandma's Marathon, at the age of 30, Kevin finished in 256th place in 2:45:29 – his personal record.

CHAPTER 12

The Voice

It was the seventh annual American Birkebeiner, a 55-kilometer cross-country ski race. The setting is in Northern Wisconsin, surrounded by the one-million-acre Chequamegon National Forest. There is abundant and diverse wildlife, beautiful, secluded county roads and forest trails carved throughout the woods.

The race starts in downtown Hayward, Wisconsin, and finishes at the Telemark Lodge, in the outskirts of the small town of Cable, with only 300 residents.

It was Saturday, February 24, 1979, and the early morning temperature was minus eight degrees, later warming to the low teens. The winds were from the east and relativity light at seven miles per hour.

The race conditions were almost ideal. The sky was clear blue, with the sun shining brightly on the pure white surface. It was a typical Wisconsin winter day with everyone dressed in heavy coats, mukluk boots and deerskin chopper mittens.

Debbie Blackmer, general manager of Grandma's Saloon and Deli, and I took the 75-mile drive to observe the race. Blackmer was always eager to help with the planning of Grandma's Marathon. We were hoping to pick up ideas we could incorporate into our event.

We packed some sandwiches and filled a large thermos with hot chocolate and headed to our neighboring state. When we arrived, we parked the car in a large-plowed field near the Telemark Lodge. We could feel the excitement as thousands of spectators strolled around outside drinking hot beverages.

The announcer was keeping everyone informed an hour or so before the lead skiers would approach the long flat straightaway to the finish. Colorful banners were draped along the fencing and flags of different countries were flying high. It was a festive setting that certainly caught our eyes and influenced us for our upcoming June race.

* * *

Tony Wise, of Norwegian heritage, founded the American Birkebeiner in 1973. Wise patterned his ski marathon after the Birkebeinerrennet, which has been held in Norway since 1932. Thirty-four men and one woman officially started the first race.

Wise was born in 1921 in Hayward and as a 26-year-old purchased a hill for $750, which later became Mount Telemark Ski Resort. Wise had another vision for his property. In December of 1972, he finished a six-million-dollar lodge and resort. It would become one of the premier upper Midwest vacation destinations during all four seasons.

As you walk into the lobby, a large, majestic fireplace immediately greets you. The smell of the burning birch logs invites you to sit in one of the oversized leather chairs and feel its warmth.

There was a beautiful indoor and outdoor swimming pool, not far from the guest check-in. The resort amenities also included fine dining restaurants, tennis courts, a golf course, bike and ski rental shops, and enough beds to sleep 650. There was even a small airport just a quarter mile from the lodge's parking lot. It became a huge economic boost to the greater Cable/Hayward area.

* * *

There were 4,459 skiers entered in the 1979 race, the largest cross-country ski event in North America.

Blackmer and I worked our way to the fenced finish area and claimed our standing position. We were 100 feet from the finish line, and a powerful, mesmerizing voice caught our attention. We were in awe of the announcer's masterfulness. He informed, educated and entertained the large crowd for hours.

Debbie and I looked at each other and almost in unison said, "We need to bring this guy to Grandma's." We had never invested in a finish line announcer but, after hearing him, we knew it needed to happen. His name was Peter Graves. Introductions were made after the race, and business cards were exchanged.

Almost four months later, on June 23, Peter was set up on raised scaffolding at the finish of Grandma's Marathon. A microphone was the tool of his trade. Peter always did his homework, knew the race favorites, course and age group records and was aware of many captivating runner stories.

Elite runners were just a small part of the race. Peter would attempt to recognize every runner approaching the finish line. His responsibilities weren't over until the last runner finished. In Peter's mind, all of the participants were champions.

Peter's endurance was amazing. He was now part of what would help make Grandma's Marathon one of the best marathons in the nation. Peter told our story to the world. He never cared to receive recognition. It was only about the athletes, fast and slow.

Peter has only missed two Grandma's Marathons since 1979. He became a mainstay and is counted on each year to be a part of our team.

* * *

Peter Graves and Michael Pinocci, finish line announcers at Grandma's Marathon.

Peter Graves was born in Bennington, Vermont, in May, 1952. His parents introduced him to cross country skiing at a young age. Peter was on the Bennington High School ski team and in 1970 was selected to be on the United States Junior National Team in Jackson Hole, Wyoming.

Peter never claimed to be a gifted skier but overcame his lack of natural talent with hard work and determination. He had a passion for the outdoors and a true love for the winter season.

For the next four years, Peter continued his education and skiing at Fort Lewis College in Durango, Colorado. As a junior, he began broadcasting reports for a local radio station. This was his start in the industry, and he soon discovered he had a talent for talking.

From 1976 to 1981, Peter was employed in Minneapolis as the marketing director for a Norwegian ski importer and began to appreciate the beauty of the Upper Midwest. The weather and people were similar to his birthplace in Vermont.

From 1981 to 1984, Peter served as the U.S. Ski Team Regional cross-country coach. In the fall of 1985, he accepted the Nordic Ski Director position at Giants Ridge in Biwabik, Minnesota, and assisted with the promotion of the World Cup race there.

Peter's résumé is long and diverse. He has traveled the world as part of a special brotherhood in the promotion of goodwill in sports. Peter has worked as a commentator or public address announcer in 11 Olympic Games – three summer and eight winter. Over the years he has developed the skills to work at almost any venue from skiing to judo.

Peter's annual pilgrimage to Duluth is a celebration, a reunion with many friends, and gives him the opportunity to enjoy a pint of his favorite beer at Fitger's Brewhouse or a short walk to the Portland Malt Shoppe.

Peter has helped elevate our events to a very high level. In 1998, he was inducted into the Grandma's Marathon Hall of Fame, and received the 2015 Ron Daws Ambassador Award for his contributions to Grandma's Marathon.

* * *

As a freshman at Washington High School in Fremont, California, Michael Pinocci joined the cross-country team. His motivation was to earn a letter jacket, but he needed to finish in the top 12 on his team. Michael finished 13th.

He then tried out for soccer but was quickly cut.

Not giving up on his goal to earn a letterman's jacket, he joined the track team in the spring of 1969 and focused on becoming a long jumper. This was cut short when the field coach, not seeing much promise, suggested that he return to distance running.

In the last two-mile race of the season at the league championship, Michael finished fifth and finally earned his jacket. That two-mile race was the beginning of a great career as an elite runner.

Michael participated in more than 30 marathons, finishing 18 in under 2:20.

Shortly after the 1984 U.S. Men's Marathon Olympic Trials in Buffalo, New York, I invited Michael to run Grandma's Marathon. He had dropped out of the race in New York, but I knew he was fit and could be a contender.

Grandma's was held on June 16, and my hunch paid off as Michael finished second in a personal best time of 2:14:02. England's Derek Stevens won in 2:12:40.

In 1985, Michael returned to Duluth and finished 14th in 2:19:51.

Shortly after the 1985 race, Michael was diagnosed with exercise-induced arrhythmia. It is the most common fitness-related arrhythmia, which often occurs in those with a high level of physical fitness. It causes a rapid and erratic heartbeat during exercise or rest. The treatment is to reduce exercise or take medication. Michael did both.

I received a call from Michael in the early months of 1986, asking if there was anything he could do to stay involved with Grandma's. It was an easy decision on my part. We had become friends and I knew he would be a great asset.

We were working Peter Graves way too much at our press conferences, finish line and award ceremony. It was time to give Peter some help and I knew Michael would be able to provide an important elite runner perspective. Michael became the assistant master of ceremonies for Grandma's Marathon. Michael has continued in that role for 35 straight years.

"It has been a big part of my life. There have been so many lasting memories, and in the most complimentary way, what I love about Duluth is, nothing changes," Michael said. "I feel indebted to Grandma's for all they have done for me. It has given me a sense of purpose and a way to reconnect with so many friends."

Michael was inducted into the Grandma's Marathon Hall of Fame in 2004 and received the 2015 Ron Daws Ambassador Award alongside Peter Graves.

CHAPTER 13

Herb Dillon

It was in early June of 1979 when Jan Paavola, the wife of my good friend Marty, asked Herb Dillon to volunteer at Grandma's Marathon. They were both registered nurses and co-workers at Saint Mary's Hospital in Duluth. Jan was organizing a small group of medical personnel to help out at the finish line.

The need for additional support was a big concern as race numbers tripled from 1978. Dillon accepted and was put in charge of triage at the medical tent. The army shelter was medium size, made of thick green canvas and retained a musty, aged smell.

The U.S. Army 477th Medical Company, a Duluth Reserve unit, was responsible for set-up and providing a dozen or so cots. The medical area was in the back parking lot of Grandma's Saloon & Deli.

This was the beginning of Herb Dillon's 42 years of volunteering for Grandma's Marathon. Dillon quickly became a fixture, providing the race the stability it needed to develop a high quality medical team.

Herb's story started in 1966 as a Duluth East High School graduate. The Vietnam War was rapidly expanding and would soon reach its peak of 550,000 U.S. troops in 1968, under President Lyndon B. Johnson. The war, considered part of the cold war era, lasted 19 years, with direct U.S. involvement ending in 1973.

Out of high school, Herb enrolled at the University of Minnesota Duluth, giving him a four-year deferment from the service. Herb stated that his enthusiasm for higher education was low and he disliked the daily regimen of classes. His grades plummeted.

During the same time, Herb found work as an orderly at St. Mary's Hospital. His responsibility was to assist nurses and other medical staff with various medical interventions. Herb loved the action of providing care to patients who needed his help. He loved working in the emergency room.

In 1969, with a little luck and help from an acquaintance, Herb transferred to the College of St. Scholastica. This was the first year the school went co-ed. Herb was accepted into the nursing program, with five male students in the first nursing class. This was the same year Herb married his wife, Sharon.

With Herb's grades at UMD being low, he was accepted, with the condition that he would be on probation for two years. He was also required to pay the first year's tuition in advance.

Herb's military deferment ended in 1971, and he joined the Army Student Nursing Corps, allowing him to continue his education at St. Scholastica. In 1973, he graduated with a nursing degree and headed to Fort Riley, Kansas, to fulfill his military obligation.

It was a small base hospital and Herb was assigned to the emergency room for the next three years.

There were 19,000 troops stationed at Fort Riley, with an additional 50,000 dependents off base. There were also many troops returning monthly from Vietnam. Herb recalls it was a nightmare, with weekly shootings and soldiers being combative, feeling they were still at war.

Herb, in an unexplainable way, enjoyed his work in trauma. He returned to Duluth in the summer of 1976, and, upon his return, St. Mary's Hospital hired him as a registered nurse in the emergency room.

This is where he wanted to be, this was his calling. After 48 years at St. Mary's, Herb retired in 2014.

While Herb does not like crowds or running, he truly enjoys being outside and became a talented race walker, who has participated in hundreds of local events.

Herb continues to volunteer for Grandma's Marathon each year and strongly feels it is a way to give back to the community.

Herb has worked closely with five different medical directors, and every one of them has counted on him to be the driving force for much of the planning.

In 1992, Herb received the Volunteer of the Year Award. In 2000, Herb was inducted into the Grandma's Marathon Hall of Fame. In 2013, a new award was created and named in Herb's honor – The Herb Dillon Medical Volunteer of the Year Award.

CHAPTER 14

Garry Bjorklund

On March 21, 1980, Jimmy Carter, the 39th President of the United States, announced that the United States was going to boycott the Summer Olympics to be held in Moscow. It was the President's form of retaliation for the 1979 Soviet invasion of Afghanistan. The United States Olympic Committee rubber-stamped the decision.

Later there was a U.S. invasion of Afghanistan following the September 11, 2001, attack on the U.S. To date, more than 2,500 U.S. Service members have died and more than 20,000 American soldiers have been wounded. In addition, there have been more than 1,700 U.S. Contractor fatalities.

When word that there would not be an Olympics for Americans in Moscow reached the country's best distance runners, a shock wave roared across the sport. Elite runners were in disbelief. Dreams were shattered.

In preparation for the 1980 Olympic Marathon Trials, Garry Bjorklund moved from Minneapolis to Boulder, Colorado, and trained from October through March, averaging from 120 to 180 miles per week. Garry was in the best shape of his life and planned to make his second Olympic team.

The Olympic Marathon Trials did take place in Buffalo, New York, on May 24, 1980. Tony Sandoval from New Mexico was crowned champion (2:10:19). Benji Durden of Colorado was second (2:10:41) and Kyle Heffner, of Colorado, was third in (2:10:55).

There was no prize money. There were no Olympics in Moscow. There was only a cheap flight back home.

A number of the best American distance runners chose not to run in Buffalo, including Bill Rodgers, Don Kardong and Garry Bjorklund. Garry was angry with Jimmy Carter. Mixing world-class athletics with politics was a sin in Garry's eyes and there was absolutely no rationale for it. He felt it was an embarrassment to our country.

After the President announced the boycott, Garry was to return to Boston in April. In 1979, he had run his personal-best time there in 2:13:14 for fifth place. Weeks later, Garry decided to cancel those plans and decided he was going to have his Olympics back home in northern Minnesota at Grandma's Marathon on June 21.

The Moscow Olympics opening ceremony was on July 19, less than a month after Grandma's. Eighty nations celebrated the joy of sports in Russia.

The stars were lining up nicely in the planning of the fourth annual Grandma's Marathon. Runners were signing up at a record pace and the excitement in the community was spirited by eager volunteers.

The city leaders were beginning to understand the importance of special events and how they could bring millions of tourism dollars to the city coffers. The support we were receiving from local businesses was incrementally growing.

The 1980 budget was $35,000 with a $5 entry fee.

1977 – 150 registered runners
1978 – 667 registered runners
1979 – 1,682 registered runners
1980 – 3,085 registered runners

The crystal ball was glowing brightly and telling us that we were going to have a great future. Even closing 26 miles of public roadway was almost becoming the norm.

In the spring of 1980, Grandma's Marathon had a press conference with Garry Bjorklund at Grandma's Saloon and Deli. In an article written afterward by Duluth News Tribune reporter, Sam

Cook, Garry was quoted as saying, "I feel that I let down the people of Duluth," referencing his second-place finish at Grandma's in 1979. "I plan to run hard here, and I hope to break the course record."

It was extremely important for me to bring Garry back in 1980. Garry was born in Duluth, raised in Twig and went to Proctor High School. His connection to his birthplace has always been strong.

Cook quoted me saying, "Garry is our main man. That he chooses to run Grandma's, and to give it maximum effort, is very significant."

Cook also quoted Garry saying, "I wanted to isolate myself in Colorado, to eat, sleep and think running. I really hoped to be on the Olympic team."

In the same article, Cook described Garry as lean, tan and strong. Garry had reduced his miles, averaging 100 to 120 per week in final preparation for the June race.

* * *

Garry ran his first marathon at the inaugural Grandma's Marathon on June 25, 1977. He was a 1976, 10,000-meter Olympian, which gave us a great deal of legitimacy right out of the chute. I privately raised $200 to give to Garry for expense money. Our total operational budget was $649.53.

The morning of the race was hot with full sun. The race started at 11 a.m. because the Saloon at the finish line wanted to be open before the runners arrived. They were hoping to recover their sponsorship money by selling food and beer. I caved in to them with that late start for that year only.

We had approximately 200 volunteers on the course at water stations and road crossings. Most of them were friends, acquaintances and family members. Marty Paavola's parents, Ray and Gerty, were the 17-mile water station captains, my brother,

Gary, was in charge of the 11-mile water station and my dad used his old beat-up Toyota truck with a mattress in the back as the sag wagon for those who couldn't finish the race.

Garry easily won that day in the horrid conditions, even after having to stop to change his shoes because of blisters. His time was 2:21:54.

* * *

Sunday, June 22, 1980, Cook wrote on his experience of going to the starting line. Cook was one of the 3,000 participants.

"The rain whipped out of gray skies and streaked windows of the old yellow school bus in oblique strips. The starting line area was a quarter mile deep with lithe, sinewy bodies hopping in place to keep warm in the morning shower.

The rain abated just before the race started as if someone more powerful than even the race director approved. The clouds parted and the sun shone brightly on the lead runners as they ascended with bright colors over the gentle hill on mile one."

The race started exactly at 9 a.m. just outside Two Harbors. Garry was in fine form with a world-class performance and a finishing time of 2:10:20. Garry broke the course record by 4 minutes and 23 seconds. It was the third- fastest marathon time run by an American. Robert Wallace from Australia finished second in 2:16:40.

The race was held in nearly ideal conditions for the elite and early finishers with a few cooling showers in the morning. However, as the day continued, it became muggy with temperatures rising into the 80s.

Seventy-five runners broke 2:40. Mark Melander of Duluth was the last runner to break three hours. He finished 388th.

Lorraine Moller from New Zealand won the women's division in 2:38:36. On August 4, 1980, just a little over a month after her victory at Grandma's, she won the Women's International

Marathon in London, in 2:35:11. She wore a pair of running shoes given to her by Garry Bjorklund.

We added a special award for the first grandmother that year, which has been a very important tradition since. Mae Horns from Edina, Minnesota captured the title at the age of 46 with a time of 3:16:59.

Garry Bjorklund becomes Grandma's Marathon champion for the second time in 1980.

In 1980, Garry Bjorklund sets the course record running a solo 2:10:20 - six minutes ahead of the second-place finisher.

Lorraine Moller of New Zealand on a warm day in 1980, wins her second Grandma's Marathon in 2:38:36.

Marcia Bevard of Duluth was the first female in the wheelchair division (2:52:57) and Russ Stover of Duluth was the first male in 3:14:52.

A wheelchair division began in 1979 at Grandma's. Jim Finch of Minneapolis (2:30:09) was the men's champion and Sharon Limpert of Minneapolis (3:11:27) was the women's winner.

In the early years of wheelchair racing, the participants used their standard day chairs. The slick and aerodynamic racing chairs came much later.

Grandma's Marathon's commitment to wheelers was an important step that helped bring recognition and opportunities to disabled athletes.

Grandma's Marathon has gone on to invite wheelers from all over the globe and the race added many thousands of dollars to the budget for transportation, lodging and prize money. It personally meant a lot to me to support these incredible athletes. Every year it was one of my most enjoyable moments watching them race.

* * *

In 1983, Garry Bjorklund married Rhonda McGrane. They chose to leave Minnesota for a fresh start in Boulder, Colorado. In 1990, they moved to Fort Collins, Colorado where they live today. The couple has two daughters, Hanna and Ella. They welcomed a new love into their life in 2019 – their first grandchild, Jack.

CHAPTER 15

Dick Beardsley

Dick Beardsley completed his first year as a cross country runner for Wayzata High School in the fall of 1973. Dick was a lean 140 pound, six-foot-tall athlete. He had the perfect physique for a distance runner. He had only been a runner for a little over three months and, during the last race of the season, he squeaked out a seventh-place finish, which earned him a spot on the varsity squad and a letterman's jacket.

This was the beginning of a marvelous journey, one that nobody, let alone himself, would have ever thought possible. The odds were one in a million.

After the cross-country season, there was pressure from his coaches and teammates to join the track team in the spring. Dick would have nothing of it. He was going to spend any free time fishing in the nearby lakes. Dick loves fishing, but more importantly he had a chance to spend some valuable time with his dad.

In the summer of 1974, Dick, 18, and fellow runner, Grant Waddell, 16, were exploring the possibility of running their first road race. They heard of a race in the middle of the woods in Northern Minnesota during the Fourth of July weekend, called the Buhl Half Marathon. The longest the two had ever run at one time was six miles.

Dick made a call to the race director, Jim Randall, who invited the two to stay with his wife and him at their home. Dick and Grant scraped up enough money for a Greyhound bus ticket to Hibbing.

On that same day, I drove with my friend, Scott Sundquist, to Jim's home. We had our sleeping bags packed and were also invited to crash on his living room floor. There were over a dozen of us staying with the Randalls' that evening.

At 7 a.m. the next morning a full school bus of runners headed to Paavola's corner, north of Buhl. The race would conclude in front of Martin Hughes High School in Hibbing.

It was a hot and humid day. Not unexpectedly, Steve Hoag from Anoka, Minnesota, easily defended his 1973 title with a time of 1:11:23. The third Buhl Half Marathon had a record number of 67 starters.

Sundquist, a North Shore Striders member, finished second in 1:14:33. I was the second Strider finisher, in ninth place in 1:20:50. Dick, who was clearly undertrained, finished 27th in 1:30:36 and Grant came in 36th in 1:39:27.

Many of us stayed for the local parade and festivities in the streets of Hibbing. Grant took the bus back to Wayzata. Dick, out of money, hitchhiked home.

Dick was developing nicely as a runner and it was only natural for him to test the waters and run his first marathon. His curiosity was high. He had a lofty goal to run the 1977 Paavo Nurmi Marathon on August 13. He had no particular goal, other than finishing.

Paavo was the most established marathon in the Upper Midwest. Many of the regional distance runners made a pilgrimage to Hurley, Wisconsin, to run the ninth annual race. Dick registered and paid his $3 entry fee.

There are always uncertainties with the marathon distance. Dick was still not properly prepared for longer distances. He had now been running for almost four years and had completed two successful cross-country seasons at the University of Minnesota Waseca under coach John Fulkrod.

The Paavo Nurmi course was challenging, and it was another hot day in Iron County. Dick ran a solid race and finished 16th in 2:47:14. He recovered quickly but was unsure of what his future would bring.

Spontaneous would be a good word to describe Dick Beardsley. Many times he reacted on emotions, and did things that weren't the best for his development as a runner. He frequently ran races on a whim.

Early in his career, he wasn't running the necessary miles he should have for the longer races. It didn't matter, he signed up anyway. He was enamored with the challenge and was beginning to develop the mentality and ego that goes along with being an elite athlete. He soon felt the power of a long-distance runner and began looking at himself as invincible.

Dick fell in love with running and was falling in love with racing – a formidable combination.

Two months after the Paavo Nurmi Marathon, Dick heard of another marathon in his own backyard – the City of the Lakes Marathon in Minneapolis. It was scheduled to take place in just five days. After signing up, Dick panicked a bit thinking, "What the heck did I just do?" Once again, he wasn't in the best shape to run 26.2 miles.

The race was run on a multiple-loop course around inner-city lakes. It was a beautiful fall morning with cool temperatures – one of those rare days that would be favorable for everyone. Dick took off with the leaders with the goal of breaking his 2:47 personal record. He was also hoping to finish in the top ten.

Dick's strategy was to run with Barney Klecker and the other notable entrants for as long as he could. He hung in the top ten and felt reasonably well until the 23-mile mark, when his legs started to buckle and he began losing stamina. Every choppy stride he took was exhausting the few ounces of energy he had left.

Dick, still inexperienced, made two disastrous mistakes. First, he didn't drink any water during the race, and second, wore a new pair of running shoes purchased the day before.

Dehydration, cramps and blood blisters were his enemy. Dick collapsed as he crossed the finish line in seventh place. He was escorted to the medical tent for evaluation and fluids. He met his goal of getting into the top ten and received a small trophy.

This was nine positions better than he finished at Paavo two months earlier in 1977.

The noteworthy story of Dick's accomplishment didn't make it into the newspaper coverage the next morning. His finish did not even raise the eyebrows of anyone at the race. Dick ran 2:33:22, improving by almost 14 minutes. In fact, this very well could have been the breakthrough moment in his running career. It was a huge improvement for someone who was under-prepared and making so many foolish mistakes.

This was very significant. He was now on the brink of becoming an elite runner.

After a few more marathons under his belt, Dick enrolled at South Dakota State in the fall of 1978. His mission was to have Scott Underwood coach him; school would be an afterthought. Dick's college days only lasted four months.

During that time, Dick began dating fellow college student, Mary Hausmann. They fell in love and were married on June 23, 1979 – the same day as the third Grandma's Marathon.

Dick kept running marathons and, astonishingly, was improving in each one. On June 17, exactly one week before his wedding day, he found himself at the starting line of the Manitoba International Marathon in Winnipeg.

He was attempting to earn a qualifying time for the 1980 Olympic Marathon Trials. When Dick crossed the finish line, the clock read 2:21:54, beating the required time by two seconds.

On May 24, 1980, Dick found himself at the Olympic Marathon Trials in Buffalo, New York. The temperature at the start was already in the mid-60s and the humidity was steadily rising. It was clear it was going to be a challenging day for the runners.

Dick was full of confidence. He had never broken 2:20 in the marathon and looked forward to testing himself with America's best distance runners. His performance didn't disappoint. He finished in 16th place, in 2:16:01, and proved to the running world that he could compete with the big boys. It was another major breakthrough.

Six marathons in nine and a half months was the path Dick took to running glory. This was the most important time of his running career and Dick's unconventional racing schedule was one that many others, including Garry Bjorklund, advised him not to take.

Dick ignored the advice. He felt great after each race – his recovery was swift, and he couldn't wait to get to his next race.

September 7, 1980: OTC Marathon – 2:15:11 – 10th place
October 26, 1980: New York Marathon – 2:13:55 – 9th place
January 10, 1981: Houston Marathon – 2:12:48 – 2nd place
February 1, 1981: Beppu Marathon, Japan – 2:12:41 – 3rd place
March 29, 1981: London Marathon – 2:11:48 – tied for 1st place
June 20, 1981: Grandma's Marathon – 2:09:37 – 1st place

CHAPTER 16

1981 – A Breakthrough Year

Saturday, June 20, 1981, was going to be a good day for many runners. The morning sky was dark grey and overcast from the late evening rains. The fog was rising in a mystic haze from Lake Superior.

The temperatures were ideal – cool with favorable northeast tailwinds.

There was a record 4,500 runners from all over the United States planning to run down Highway 61.

The competition was the best assembled in the five-year history of Grandma's Marathon. Everyone who followed the sport knew the race was going to come down to Garry Bjorklund, the 1980 champion (2:10:20), and Dick Beardsley, who had just run 2:11:48 in London three months earlier. The other invited runners would be battling for a place in the top ten.

Honorary starter, Bill Andberg, of Anoka, Minnesota, would fire the starting gun at 9 a.m.

* * *

This year also marked a major change in the racecourse. Due to the growth of the race, we no longer had enough roadway to safely stage the start and were forced to move one mile closer to Duluth. To accommodate the change, we moved the course further down Superior Street to Fifth Avenue West. Runners would follow the roadway around the Duluth Arena and reconnect to the final straightaway where thousands of spectators would be lining the street.

The last quarter mile is one of the most spectacular finishes in road racing, with the world-famous Aerial Lift Bridge standing tall as a backdrop. The sounds and sights of the active waterfront and the busy port are breathtaking. With Lake Superior so close, many runners soak their sore legs in the cold waters after crossing the finish line.

Another significant moment in 1981 was christening the largest hill on the course as "Lemon Drop Hill," named after the Lemon Drop Restaurant that sat at the crest. The base of the hill is located at mile 22. Many runners would agree it's not an ideal location for a major rise in a marathon course. It seemed fitting that it should have an appropriate name, like that of the infamous Heartbreak Hill at mile 20.5 of the Boston Marathon.

The first use of Lemon Drop Hill in print appeared in a Kevin Pates 1981 article in the post-race edition of the Duluth News Tribune. A 1983 Grandma's Marathon picture shows runners ascending the hill with the restaurant's large marquee in full view saying, " Lemon Drop Hill, it's all downhill from here!"

History sometimes gets lost with time, but the hill has now become legend, and when the legend becomes fact, print the legend. Thank you, Kevin Pates, for naming our famous hill.

* * *

In the 1981 Grandma's Marathon, Dick Beardsley (left) and Garry Bjorklund, sharing a cup of water along the course.

The 1981 race developed as most people predicted. It was a two-man race between Garry Bjorklund and Dick Beardsley. Aid stations were placed every three miles and at one station both runners were seen sharing the same paper cup of water along a portion of the North Shore.

Before the race, Garry told the media he wasn't the favorite to win. It was Dick's race to win, and he would help him with the pace as long as he could. Garry was telling the truth. He only had six weeks of preparation before race day and was noticeably more brawny than in 1980.

Garry continued to assist Beardsley on the course, instructing him to run the tangents properly. Early in the race, Dick began suffering from a side stitch, and Garry backed off the pace, allowing Dick to recover.

Garry was exactly what Dick needed on that early foggy morning. The two were on a 2:09 marathon pace, reaching the halfway point in 1:04:36.

At mile 19, on London Road Dick picked up the pace and ran a 4:42 mile. At mile 20 he continued surging with a 4:37 mile. Dick was now in full control, pulling away from Garry.

Dick was unaware of his exact pace as he entered downtown Duluth. The crowds were immense on both sides of the street, cheering him to the finish line. When he made the final turn, he could hear race announcer Peter Graves excitedly declaring that Dick was going to set a course record and break 2:10. In disbelief, Dick looked up at the clock as he approached the finish line and saw 2:09.

Like a high school long jumper bounding down the final stretch, Dick crossed the finish line with a huge smile on his face and arms raised in victory. It was a spectacular race. He finished in 2:09:36.6.

His wife, Mary, mom and dad, and two sisters ran into the finishing chutes to embrace him. Everyone was in tears, including myself.

Staff Photo by Bruce Bisping

Dick Beardsley of Excelsior won Grandma's Marathon in 2 hours, 9 minutes, 36 seconds — the second-fastest clocking for an American in any marathon.

Dick Beardsley (1981) crosses the finish line in triumph, running a personal best and a Grandma's Marathon course record, 2:09:37.

Garry held on for second place in 2:11:32. Dick has often told me he felt that Garry's 2:11 performance, which he achieved in marginal marathon condition at best, surpassed his 2:09 finish. It was amazing to him that Garry could run so fast in less-than-ideal shape.

Top 10 Male Finishers - 1981
Dick Beardsley, Excelsior, MN – 2:09:37
Garry Bjorklund, Minneapolis, MN – 2:11:32
Robert Wallace, Australia – 2:13:15
Ricky Wilde, England – 2:14:42
Steve Benson, Bloomington, MN – 2:14:42
Matt Wilson, Fairfax, VA – 2:14:46
Rick Callison, Piqua, OH – 2:15:11
Barney Klecker, Hopkins, MN – 2:15:20
Tony Shockency, St. Paul, MN – 2:16:59
Bob Hensley, Milford, CT – 2:17:00

Seventeen runners broke 2:20. There was no prize money.

Dick's 2:09:37 course record stood for 33 years until Dominic Ondoro of Kenya broke it in 2014 when he ran 2:09:06.

Top 10 Female Finishers – 1981
Lorraine Moller, New Zealand – 2:29:36
Janice Horns, Edina, MN – 2:36:47
Janice Ettle, St. Cloud, MN – 2:42:47
Mary Bange, LaCrosse, WI – 2:44:14
DeeAnn Dougherty, Rochester, MN – 2:54:03
Georgette Green, Houston, TX – 2:56:37
Evelyn Cowan, Sun Prairie, WI – 2:57:43
Kathleen Kapalin, Green Bay, WI – 2:58:00
Karen Thomas, La Crosse, WI – 2:58:58
Lisa Berry Moore, Milwaukee, WI – 2:59:42

Eleven runners broke three hours. There was no prize money.

Lorraine Moller (1981) accepts her 1st place award after setting a Grandma's Marathon course record (2:29:35).

Lorraine Moller's 2:29:36 course record stood for 18 years until Elena Makolova of Belarus broke it when she ran 2:29:12 in 1999.

* * *

There were many great performances that morning, including by Bill Andberg, aka the "Grey Ghost", the official race starter. After Bill fired the gun, he handed it to a volunteer and ran the race.

He was 70, the oldest runner in the event. In his running career, he set 30 age group national and world records at a variety of distances. Bill finished the 1981 marathon in style, beating more than 2,000 runners in 3:30:25.

Andberg was always invited to be a part of Grandma's Marathon and for many years handed out awards in the Big Top Tent, kissing all of the honored women on the cheek.

Bill died on December 11, 2007, at 96.

* * *

Dr. Alex Ratelle of Edina, Minnesota, finished his 101st marathon in Duluth. Alex, 56, ran 2:30:39 that day. It was an American men's record for the 55-59 age group, which stood for six years. He finished in 69th place, only five spots behind Lorraine Moller, the women's champion.

* * *

Barney Klecker was getting ready to drive 150 miles on Interstate 35 to Duluth from his townhouse in Hopkins. It was early in the morning before race day, and in a frenzy, he slipped in his stocking feet and fell down the stairs, breaking the second and third toes on his right foot. It was intensely painful, and he was barely able to get his shoe on.

Barney was in the best shape of his marathon career and was confident he would run the race of his lifetime. He was training hard, averaging 150 miles per week the last six months.

Before Grandma's Marathon, Barney chose to run the 1981 Boston Marathon on April 21st. He was fit and ready to go. At the

Boston halfway point he was overcome by a side stitch and had to slow back to a recreational pace. With ten kilometers to go the pain subsided and he began to zoom past hundreds of runners. He ran the last 10K in 30:10, and finished 28th in 2:16, just one place behind Doug Kurtis.

His attention turned to training to run 2:10 or 2:11 at Grandma's.

The trip to Duluth was long and painful because of the broken toes. Barney had doubts about being able to run the next morning. He picked up his race packet, hobbled back to his room at the Radisson Hotel, and was afraid to take off his shoe.

I happened to be at the Radisson at the same time and we both went to Dr. Alex Ratelle's room to seek advice. After some gentle maneuvering, the shoe finally came off. It didn't look good. His toes were bent inward and had a deep black and blue tone. I found a large bucket and filled it with ice and cold water, and Barney reluctantly submerged his foot.

Dr. Ratelle's assessment was that Barney could run in the morning if he was willing to endure the pain. I was skeptical.

In the early morning hours, Barney took three Anacin-3 pain pills. At the starting line he took three more and carried three additional pills in his pocket for later.

At the start, Barney recruited a good friend, Mike Seaman, to stand on his right side. He wanted to make sure no one would accidentally step on his injured toes.

There was a pack of a dozen runners at ten miles, still within sight of Bjorklund and Beardsley. The pace was fast. They ran 50:18 for the first ten miles, which was a personal record for many of them.

Barney's training was paying off. He was running comfortably and within his ability. As he approached London Road at mile 19, his right foot began flaring up and the pain was becoming unbearable. He could see blood seeping through his light colored nylon shoe.

The last seven miles were the hardest of his life. Most runners would have dropped out. Actually, most runners would have never started the race.

Barney finished eighth with a personal best marathon time of 2:15:20. The grimace on his face as he crossed the finish line was a look of pain that I had never seen before and hope not to see again.

In the medical tent, volunteers were forced to cut Barney's shoe off. His sock was blood-soaked, and his toes were swollen. As he sat there, Barney reminisced about what he could have run on that perfect day without two broken toes.

Barney, John, and Janis Klecker during a recent trip to Duluth.

CHAPTER 17

Boston Bound

The Deluxe Coney Island on West First Street in Duluth is always a great place for locals to grab a quick lunch. As you enter the front door, the aroma of the coney sauce immediately hits your nostrils. The hotdogs cook tightly side-by-side in multiple rows on the flat top grill. There is a container full of fresh, finely chopped onions next to it.

My intention every time I go is to buy two coneys, light on the onions, and a Coke. However, when it's my turn to order, I always end up buying three.

It's an old, narrow and long building with worn out tables and booths taking most of the space in the back, and a modest salad bar up front. With my tray in hand, I head directly to the dining counter with the spinning circular stools bolted to the floor. A newspaper is always scattered about. My spot is directly in front of the malt machine, where you can't help notice the old sign on the wall that proclaims:

Not even a fish would
get in trouble if it
didn't open its mouth.

* * *

Shortly after the 1981 race, news spread that the brother of marathon star Bill Rodgers declared our course was short and the times were inaccurate.

I never met Charlie Rodgers and I am almost positive he has never been to Duluth. I found his accusations reckless and unwarranted. It was offensive to everyone who ran in the race, but I knew his comments were directly aimed at Dick Beardsley. Dick had just run the fourth fastest marathon in the world that year.

We had the official certificate of the measurements from the national governing body. An authorized and respected road racing professional had measured the course, and it was indeed accurate. But, in mid-July we measured it again to further prove Grandma's Marathon was legitimate. The results were the same. The course was 26.2 miles.

Unfortunately, one person's words can be so damaging. I have an open invitation for Charlie Rodgers to visit Duluth. If he ever takes me up on it, I will be glad to buy him three coneys and a Coke and sit with him in front of the sign at the Deluxe Coney Island.

* * *

It was late fall on the West Bank of Minneapolis in 1981. Reservations were made for an evening dinner with Dick and Mary Beardsley. I was anxious, knowing this would be my one and only opportunity to make my pitch to Dick for his return to Grandma's.

Dick was going to run the Boston Marathon on April 19, 1982. His races and training were being designed and planned by coach Bill Squires. Dick was determined to take his running to the next level.

My goal was to get Dick's commitment to be our headliner in 1982. I had a written agreement in my briefcase and Dick was aware that this was a business dinner. We were both uncomfortable talking about money and our conversation was full of small talk as though we had never met before.

I explained to him how Duluth had adopted him and, after his win at Grandma's, he had become a hometown hero. Dick always had a difficult time saying no to race directors. He is fair-minded and I felt deep in my heart he wanted to return. A few minutes into my pitch, I made my best offer:

- $75 for food
- $100 for travel
- $3,500 for appearance money
- 3-nights lodging at the Radisson Hotel

Dick put his hand out immediately and we shook. The agreement was signed on the spot.

* * *

Prize money for men and women was first awarded at Grandma's in 1989. Most elite runners in the early days were lucky to receive a modest shoe contract for free gear. Race directors may have given them a complimentary entry, some food money and a place to sleep.

Up to my retirement in 2013, Grandma's Marathon invested more than $2.1 million in prize money. We spent an equal amount in bonus, transportation, food and lodging monies. I was committed to helping elite runners.

* * *

After my meeting with Dick, I purchased an airline ticket to Boston for the 1982 Boston Marathon. There was no way on earth I would miss Dick's run there. I secured a hotel room downtown, thanks to a company called Marathon Tours.

The Boston Athletic Association (BAA) provided me with a general credential, which I soon found out provided little access to anything. I was happy to put something around my neck though so I could at least look official.

Early in 1982, Dick left the cold and snowy Minnesota winter to train in Atlanta where the temperatures were more mild. Coach Squires' plan was to have Dick train on the hilly roads in Georgia that mimicked the Boston Marathon course.

Alberto Salazar, a Wayland, Massachusetts native, was coming back from Oregon to run the race. It would be his third marathon and first attempt at Boston. This was his town and he was favored to win. In his debut marathon in 1980, Salazar won the New York City Marathon in 2:09:41. He followed it up in New York in 1981 with a world record time of 2:08:13. Salazar was not accustomed to losing races of any length.

Bill Rodgers, a Bostonian and a four-time Boston Marathon champion, would be wearing race number one. In 1979, Rodgers ran 2:09:27 at Boston for the fastest marathon time in the world that year. No one in the race knew how to run this course better than "Boston Billy".

* * *

The Boston Marathon is always held on Patriots Day, the third Monday in April. It became a state holiday in 1894. The race is on a point-to-point course and begins in Hopkinton, a small town of 16,000 people. The finish is in front of the Prudential Tower in downtown Boston.

This was my first time there and, as a good tourist, I took the opportunity to visit the Old North Church, Faneuil Hall Marketplace and Legal Seafood for a bowl of clam chowder. The history of the city and the food were stunning. I fell in love with Boston.

On the morning of the race, I was up at the crack of dawn to watch the crew set up the finish line area. I was in awe of how professional everything was. The amount of money they spent on bleachers, scaffolding and all of the amenities would have easily exceeded our total budget. It was breathtaking and I was in heaven observing every detail.

The best spot to watch the race was on the bleachers located only a few yards in front of the beautiful gold and blue painted finish. I climbed up and sat halfway in the center for the best view. I was there all by myself with no security in sight.

There were four large television screens stretched out in front with portable bathrooms on either side. I sat there for hours watching the final assembly of the equipment, with commotion everywhere. As time went on, it became clear that I was not supposed to be on those bleachers, which I later learned were called “The Governor’s Stand” and were reserved for city and state dignitaries. A policeman escorted in the Bishop, Governor, Mayor, Chief of Police, BAA board members, and dozens of others to their seats around me.

As the bleachers continued to fill up, the woman to my left was Grandma Salazar. The entire Salazar clan filled the rest of the row. Alberto was on the minds of everyone, except for me. I was silently cheering for Dick.

Salazar wore number two and Dick had number three. This was the 86th running of the race and there was no prize or appearance money offered.

I talked to Grandma Salazar throughout the race. She knew I was from Minnesota, and I explained to her that Dick had won our race the past June. She very kindly told me, “If Alberto doesn’t win, I hope Dick does.” I replied instantly, “Well, if Dick doesn’t win, I hope Alberto does!”

With nine miles left to go in the race, the rest of the pack had dropped off and it was just Dick and Salazar running neck-and-neck. The question on everybody’s mind was who would have the leg speed in the final stretch.

Salazar didn’t take a drop of water the entire race. He even declined Dick’s offer to share his cup as Garry Bjorklund had done during the 1981 Grandma’s.

The crowds were thick, at least ten rows deep. The two leaders weaved in and out of view from behind the police motorcycle escorts.

In the end, the race became an American classic with Salazar, 23, pulling ahead with just 40 yards to go. He crossed the finish line in first place edging Dick, 26, by two seconds.

Salazar won his third marathon in a row with a time of 2:08:51. Dick set another personal best time of 2:08:53. After crossing the finish line, Salazar was visibly cold and shaking and his eyes were glazed over. Volunteers at the finish line quickly covered him with blankets. Both runners embraced each other, exhausted and emotional. It was the race of a lifetime for both and a magical day for everyone who watched.

Shortly after a brief ceremony at the finish line, a police escort came to take the Salazar family to the underground parking ramp in the Prudential Building where the press conference would be held. I remained sitting as they shuffled past when Grandma Salazar turned and said, "Scott, you are with us." I followed blindly.

Dick was the only runner at the conference. Salazar was not doing well. The Boston Marathon medical team worked diligently to save his life. The combination of the blistering 4:55 per mile pace, the heat during the race, the hilly course and not staying hydrated had taken a toll.

Watching the battle between Dick and Salazar, which would be dubbed "The Duel In The Sun", with Grandma Salazar by my side is a memory I will carry forever.

* * *

Dick's recovery after Boston was more challenging than he had ever experienced. Not wanting to back out of his commitment to me to run Grandma's Marathon on June 21, 1982, he began to train again, instead of letting his body fully recover. In hindsight, this marked the beginning of Dick's downfall as an elite runner.

Dick had aspirations of continuing his winning streak and running faster times. In his own eyes, he was invincible, and many people in his inner circle felt the same way, including me.

I flew Dave Babiracki in from California to pace Dick in 1982. Dave was a notable runner who had run 1:02:56 in the half marathon. I was caught up in the hype of the possibility that Dick could set a world record at Grandma's.

The temperature at the start that year was 56 degrees, with partly cloudy skies and light precipitation. It was a good day for a race.

However, the cards were stacked against Dick. He was tired, and Babiracki fell off the pace early. There was no Garry Bjorklund to push him, and we didn't have the depth of competition that he needed.

Dick won his second Grandma's with a respectable time of 2:14:49. He crossed the finish line with a smile on his face, but only because he was glad to have finished. Matt Wilson from Fairfax, Virginia was second in 2:16:10.

* * *

Dick Beardsley holds on for victory in the 1982 Grandma's Marathon (2:14:49). His winning time comes just two months after his famous duel with Alberto Salazar at the Boston Marathon.

Dick ran seven more marathons after his 1982 Grandma's. His fastest time in that stretch was March 8, 1987, when he won the Napa Valley Marathon in 2:16:20.

Dick was inducted into the Grandma's Marathon Hall of Fame in 1998, and continues to be one of the race's greatest ambassadors.

CHAPTER 18

Friend or Foe

The Grandma's Marathon racecourse from Two Harbors to Duluth has changed very little over the years, mainly because there are not many options for change.

The Minnesota Department of Transportation (MnDOT) has been superlative in their support for delaying road construction and bridge replacement projects so the race could be held. This support is imperative for the race. This doesn't mean there haven't been difficulties and challenges in the past years with the agency.

The construction and final extension of I-35 took almost three decades of planning. I-35 is a north/south highway that stretches 1,593 miles from Duluth, Minnesota to Laredo, Texas.

The dates of my meetings in the early months of 1983 with John Pawlak, district one engineer of MnDOT, are a little fuzzy in my memory. The content of the meetings, however, is not.

I was in my early 30s and he had been working as the district engineer since his appointment in 1971. Pawlak, 70, was close to retiring.

I must have certainly seemed like a young punk with an audacious personality. I needed to be firm and steadfast, as the future of Grandma's Marathon was in his hands.

As sections of I-35 were being completed through Duluth, John Pawlak was on record stating that Grandma's Marathon would not be able to continue in its present form. His position was clear. He would never close a portion of the interstate to accommodate a running race.

My meetings were unsuccessful, and it looked like Grandma's Marathon would suffer a quick and painful death.

After my second tense meeting, the local media were waiting for comment as I departed MnDOT's Mesaba Avenue headquarters. My response was harsh, saying Pawlak had no vision, and he was unable to see the economic importance of Grandma's Marathon to Duluth and the surrounding area. He was stubborn and uncooperative in every way. I gave the media great talking points for the evening newscast.

I was taking the underdog position and characterizing Pawlak as the bully. This was clearly my strategy, but I wasn't counting on it working.

My second plan of action was similar to my 1977 meeting with Air Force Colonel Gatlin. This time I would write a one-page letter to Minnesota Governor Rudy Perpich and attempt to go over Pawlak's head to plead my case to his boss.

I never received a direct response from Governor Perpich, but I knew Pawlak did. The conflict between us disappeared and Grandma's Marathon became the first running event in the nation to close down a portion of an interstate highway.

Dave Ekern, a Pawlak successor, described him as a no-nonsense person in his management style. Pawlak was always willing to share his thoughts on all issues and was committed to do what he believed to be the right thing. It seemed clear in his mind that supporting a major running event in his own backyard was not the right thing to do.

Pawlak retired on December 31, 1983, and Rudy Perpich appointed John Sandahl as the new District One MnDOT Engineer on February 8, 1984. This was a gift from the heavens.

John Bray, who was the special assistant to the district engineer, described one of Sandahl's first staff meetings. He let everyone know that he was planning to make a number of important changes in the general philosophy of how the agency thought about and worked with special events. District One would become a partner and work closely with athletic organizations like Grandma's Marathon in every possible way.

This was one of the most important days in the history of Grandma's Marathon. Sandahl and his staff of engineers would now plan construction around our race.

Bray further described Sandahl as a pure diplomat who would always take the time to listen to his staff before making important decisions. For the first time, MnDOT was a strong community ally.

On October 28, 1992, Gary Doty, the mayor of Duluth, cut the ribbon at the 1480 foot long Leif Erikson tunnel to signify the completion of the final phase of the I-35 extension. The total cost of the project was $200,345,000.

The battle with Pawlak wasn't one I wanted, but it was one I had no choice but to fight. I was advocating for the future of special events in Northeastern Minnesota. In my mind it was extremely important that government appointees and elected officials become positive partners in the growth of tourism, not adversaries.

* * *

Rudy Perpich was a compassionate and understanding Governor who became a regular fixture at our finish line and award ceremonies.

In 2006, we honored Governor Perpich with a public service award in his name. The purpose is to recognize public employees each year for their extraordinary service and contributions to Grandma's Marathon.

CHAPTER 19

The Jenny Spangler Story

This is a story about a teenage runner from Rockford, Illinois, a mid-size city, with slightly less than 150,000 residents. It is located in the northern part of the state, approximately 90 miles northwest of Chicago.

Jenny Spangler is modest and humble and has a warm and inviting persona. If you ever have a chance to meet her you will instantly be overwhelmed by her kindness and become a friend and a fan.

Jerry Hassard, coach of the track and cross-country teams at the University of Iowa, worked hard to recruit Jenny as a scholarship athlete. During her campus visit in the early winter months of 1981, she fell in love with Iowa's academic programs and Hassard's coaching philosophy. There was no doubt in her mind she'd be moving to Iowa City in the fall.

Academics would be Jenny's main priority, but her running career wouldn't be far behind.

From a young age, Jenny enjoyed the serenity of running longer distances. She was inspired by watching the Rockford Marathon and, in the back of her mind, she knew she'd attempt the distance in the near future. However, this dream was put on hold as she packed her bags and headed to the Hawkeye state for her freshman year as a member of Iowa's highly competitive NCAA Division 1 cross country team.

By the spring of 1983, Jenny became an All-American 10,000-meter track runner, setting a personal record of 33:39. She had become one of the best female distance runners in the United States.

Coach Hassard was aware of Jenny's burning desire to run a marathon. She was in phenomenal shape and if she could run 2:51:16 she would qualify for the first Women's Olympic Marathon Trials in Olympia, Washington in 1984. That was her goal.

The marathon dream was flowing deeply through her veins. Jenny and coach Hassard sought advice from members of the Iowa City Striders, and she gradually increased her long runs to 20 miles. She averaged 60 miles per week, which is considered a modest amount for a competitive marathoner.

Jenny received numerous recommendations by members of the Iowa City Striders to run Grandma's Marathon on June 11. The timing was perfect. She needed to run a marathon in late spring or early summer in order to achieve the qualifying standard and not interfere with the start of the cross-country season in August.

In late May, I received a phone call from coach Hassard explaining he had a young and talented runner who wanted to qualify for the Olympic Trials at Grandma's. He described Jenny's marathon potential and that she was one of the fastest collegiate distance runners in the nation.

I agreed to provide her with a complimentary entry in the already full field of 7,000 runners. Lodging was found at the Edgewater Motel, a quarter mile west of the crest of the legendary Lemon Drop Hill at mile 22. Jenny's race number was 7024.

Jenny returned to Rockford a week before the race in Duluth to complete her final taper. Her parents, Carl and Helen, took her on the six-hour journey north to the last port city on the Great Lakes. Upon their arrival in Duluth, Grandma's Marathon Big Top tents at the finish line were standing tall and thousands of plates of spaghetti were being served.

After taking in the pre-race activities on the eve of the race, Jenny, her parents and coach Hassard drove the racecourse. Jenny wanted to become familiar with the terrain and landmarks of the point-to-point course. After the lengthy drive down Highway 61, she recalls her mother saying in an alarming tone, "Are you really going to run this far?" Jenny responded by saying, "I guess so."

Early Saturday morning, thousands of runners were beginning to line up at the starting line. Many were pushing forward and maneuvering as close as they could to the front – not Jenny though. She was content to start near the back. Maybe she was a little intimidated by the crowds or maybe she underestimated her ability.

The temperature at the start was already in the mid-60s and would warm to 75 degrees by noon.

When the gun fired, Jenny carefully weaved through thousands of runners as she worked her way closer to the front.

At mile nine, Jenny caught the lead woman, Lisa Larsen, 21, from Ann Arbor, Michigan. Lisa and Jenny were fierce competitors in college. In fact, Lisa beat Jenny by one position in the National Track Championship in Houston just weeks before Grandma's.

They were surprised to see each other in the race, and it was now down to the two of them. To win they would need to run the race of their lives.

Coach Hassard was a great cheerleader at the checkpoints along the course. Hassard wasn't an experienced marathon coach, but read somewhere that an energy boost was needed after the halfway point. At mile 16, Jenny's coach handed her a Snickers bar and told her to eat it. Jenny thought milk chocolate, caramel and peanuts didn't seem like a wise thing to consume and try to digest while she was racing. The Snickers bar was tossed in the ditch along the roadway.

After the race, an article by Steve Riley appeared in the Daily Iowan, an independent newspaper of the University of Iowa. Jenny was quoted, "I just kept saying to myself, 'She's not going to beat me.' She beat me at Nationals and I was still kind of mad about that."

In the same article coach Hassard described Jenny as having run "very aggressively throughout the race." She followed about five women at three miles, then at six miles she followed just one – Lisa Larsen. She sat on Lisa's shoulder from nine miles to 16, and then took the lead.

In the last two miles through downtown Duluth, thousands of spectators were cheering. Jenny said, " There were so many people and they were screaming 'It's the first woman!'"

Jenny won in 2:33:51. Lisa finished second in 2:35:03.

Gerald Helme, 25, from England won the men's race in 2:12:09. Sixty-eight runners broke two hours and thirty minutes.

Jenny beat her goal by 17 minutes and 25 seconds to qualify for the trials. She had no expectations when she started the race, and never hit the imaginary wall at mile 20. Even more impressive, Jenny's time was a world record for women age 20 and younger. The world record has since been broken, but her Grandma's time still stands as an American record. This stunning road racing record is the longest standing record in the country for men and women.

In addition, Jenny is still the second youngest marathon champion in Grandma's Marathon history. The Iowa junior was 19 at the time. Hassard died in 2012 at age 61.

* * *

Jenny Spangler of Rockford, Illinois, sets a world age group record for females 19 and under at the 1983 Grandma's Marathon (2:33:52).

Jenny is intelligent, shy, and caring, and listens more than she talks. However, there is definitely another side of her when in competition. Jenny is a shark and would have no problem shredding a competitor to pieces and spitting them out during any race. She is intense and relentless.

After a race, she will once again become your best friend, and her innocent smile will shine for many days after.

* * *

The Jenny Spangler story took another twist and she once again surprised the running world during the 1996 Women's Olympic Marathon Trials held on February 10 in Columbia, South

Carolina. This was 13 years after her world record run at Grandma's Marathon.

Jenny wore number 61, meaning 60 other runners had a faster qualifying time. She wasn't even considered a dark horse in the race. In fact, most of the other participants and spectators didn't know who she was.

Going back to 1988, Jenny had reached a level of discontent with her sport. She was exhausted mentally and physically, and running had become a chore. She had lost her love for it.

On May 1, 1988, Jenny was on the starting line of the Women's Olympic Marathon Trials in Pittsburg. She didn't want to be there and was wishing the race was over. Jenny just wanted to go back home and rest.

She finished the race in 49th place in 2:44:59.

For six years after the 1988 Trials, she ran casually for general fitness. She also earned a Masters in Business Administration degree, worked as an IT programmer and got a divorce.

After reading and seeing highlights of the 1992 Women's Marathon Trials, Jenny was contemplating a possible comeback. There was a tiny spark beginning to reignite her interest. She thought just maybe she could do it one more time.

Willie Rios, a 1500-meter Olympian from Puerto Rico living in Chicago, called Jenny and invited her to join his running group. She hesitated, but finally agreed. Her goal was to qualify for the 1996 Olympic Marathon Trials. Serious training began in the summer of 1995.

Two months before the 1996 Trials, Jenny moved to Los Angeles to escape the cold in Illinois. She joined the Santa Monica Track Club. Nine-time Olympic Gold Medalist, Carl Lewis, the club's most prominent member, paid for a small apartment for Jenny and other athletes during their stay in LA.

Jenny was now under the careful eyes of Joe Douglas, coach and founder of the club. Douglas was known as one of the great track minds in the history of the sport.

The racecourse in Columbia was difficult, with challenging hills. The temperature during the race was in the low 70s. There were 100-plus starters.

Jenny at the age of 32 was a little surprised to find herself with the lead pack as the race unfolded. She remained confident, and was very quiet, not engaging in any chitchat with her competitors.

This was becoming Jenny's race as she ran strong and bounded up the hills with rhythmic ease. Linda Somers and Anne Marie Lauck were puzzled about this runner wearing number 61.

At mile 16, Jenny made a bold move by increasing her pace to under 5:30 per mile. She was beginning to have a substantial lead on the two race favorites.

I was on the course that day and at about 17 miles I witnessed Jenny taking a sharp left turn and charge up a steep hill with no other runners in sight. Her stride going up was effortless.

I stated to the others with me that the leader was Jenny Spangler from Illinois. She was our 1983 Grandma's Marathon champion. No one else had a clue who she was.

Jenny ran alone the last ten miles of the race. Some people felt she was foolish, but the truth was they didn't know Jenny and her internal drive to win. Jenny was a courageous runner and, with two miles to go, she was confident of making the Olympic team.

She proudly broke the finish line in 2:29:54. Somers finished second in 2:30:06 and Lauck was third in 2:31:18. The winning prize was $45,000.

* * *

Jenny Spangler breaks away from the pack at the 1996 Olympic Trials, Columbia, SC. Her victory surprised the running world (2:29:54).

Jenny's running career was plagued with many injuries. She has a high arch and was a drastic toe runner, which strained her Achilles tendons after races. Stress fractures, broken bones and bone spurs were common.

Jenny's recovery after the trials was slow and she was forced to quit running because of the injuries.

From 1996 to 2003, Jenny's career as an elite distance runner was essentially over. She was recovering from surgeries, working full-time and in 2001 became pregnant with her only child, Kelli.

After the birth of her daughter, Jenny began to run again and was hoping to regain her competitive form. In the fall of 2003, once again she surprised the running world by setting an American masters record at the Chicago Marathon in 2:32:38 – at age 40.

Jenny ranks among America's all-time great runners, having set two national records and a world record.

In 1987, she was inducted into the University of Iowa Track and Field Hall of Fame. In 2007, she was inducted in the Road Runners Club of America (RRCA) Hall of Fame.

CHAPTER 20

1,039 Free Beers

I ran Grandma's Marathon in 1986. It seemed the thing to do for our 10th anniversary. I was going to have fun with it and I worked out a special promotion with our beer sponsor. They would give one extra beer ticket at the finish line for every runner who finished ahead of me.

On race morning, I wore a faded orange cotton Cambridge Sports Union (Boston Running Club) singlet given to me by my friend, Scott Sundquist. On the back I had these words printed:

I'll buy you a beer if you finish ahead of me!

During the race many runners thanked me for the beer offer. I was in average shape, running only 40 miles a week with no long runs in my preparation. I found it difficult to train properly for a race I was organizing.

I finished 1,040th in 3:13:45. I was 32 years old. There were 4,401 finishers that day. Dorothy and Sherri Spencer held a white finish line tape for me to break. It said in big black letters:

The Free Beer Stops Here

In 1986, Scott Keenan bought all 1,039 people that finished ahead of him a beer.

The afternoon award ceremony was in the Big Top Tent. I have a picture of me wearing my medallion, with Governor Rudy Perpich smiling in the background. This was the first year we provided medals to all finishers. Wells Fargo had become a sponsor and part of their agreement was to purchase them for us. It was the beginning of a very long and enjoyable relationship with the bank.

Scott Keenan poses for a photo at the 1986 award ceremony with Governor Rudy Perpich in the background.

This was shaping up to become a great day, but things quickly took a turn for the worst. Shortly after the award ceremony I was informed that a car had hit one of our young water station volunteers along the racecourse. She was taken to the hospital with a severe foot injury.

I cried when I found out and was deeply saddened for months. This was one of the most devastating things to happen in my 37 years with Grandma's Marathon.

Then at 6:20 p.m., just a few hours after finding out about the accident, tornado strength winds whipped up off of the southern shores of Lake Superior and ripped through Canal Park. The large circus tent, band equipment, tables and fencing were all gone – floating somewhere in the big lake. Large beer kegs rolled freely at high speeds through the parking lot where the tent had been just moments before. Power lines were down and sparking everywhere in the pools of rainwater.

I was at the Radisson Hotel when the storm hit. I remember seeing a steel 55-gallon garbage can flying down West Superior Street. I called Grandma's Restaurant to find out the damage, and was told all of the tents and equipment were gone.

It was a true miracle that no one was injured. The timing of the storm definitely saved lives as the race, afternoon award ceremony and live bands were finished. The large crowds had dispersed an hour before.

Needless to say, there was no Saturday evening dancing in Canal Park. The celebration was over for 1986.

* * *

In 1986, tornado-like winds destroyed the large tents near the finish line at approximately 6:20PM. There were no injuries.

About a month or so after the disastrous ending to the 1986 weekend, Andy Borg, president of Grandma's Saloon & Deli told me the restaurant was no longer going to be the major sponsor of the race. This was a total shock to me, but I managed to keep my cool and agreed to leave my office in Grandma's Corporate Building within two months.

My next move was to take a deep breath and start the transition. The first decision to make was how to operate the business. I could start my own company and own the marathon, or I could create a Minnesota nonprofit organization.

I decided to go with the nonprofit option, filed the paperwork and appointed a 17-person board of directors who were mainly friends of mine. I trademarked the name Grandma's Marathon along with the logo.

Grandma's Corporate's politically correct explanation to the public about severing ties with the marathon was that the race was getting too big and would be better off becoming more of a community event. They said it needed more freedom than being quasi-owned by the restaurant.

I was never directly told the true reason for the departure, but I knew there was more to it.

The accident on the racecourse ended up in a lawsuit and became a huge legal liability. The storm damage was costly and it certainly opened the restaurant's eyes to the risk involved in the marathon business.

I was also getting aggressive in bidding for, and being awarded, the Women's National Marathon Championships in 1987. The price tag would be another $75,000 of expenses, raising the budget to more than $300,000. There was no doubt I was beginning to make them nervous.

The end result was that the community rose to the occasion and came to my aid. Sponsorship dollars increased dramatically and gaining 100 percent independence allowed the race to grow and focus our energy solely on what was beneficial to our participants.

Grandma's Restaurant continues to be a partner of the marathon to this day, providing property and other valuable resources.

CHAPTER 21

Steve Harrington

In the fall of 1968, Steve Harrington, a senior at Windom High School, participated in the Minnesota High School Cross Country State Meet with six teammates.

Windom, a rural farming community, has a population of fewer than 4,000 residents. It was incorporated as a village in 1875 and is a part of Cottonwood County, located in the southernmost part of Minnesota, 30 miles from the Iowa border.

Garry Bjorklund, a senior at Proctor High School, was also in the race. The Twig native easily won, defeating Tom Steiner of Alexander Ramsey High School by 14 seconds. Garry's time was 9:23.9

Windom finished 15th out of 19 teams. Steve and his teammates each broke 11-minutes that day for the 2-mile race.

Steve participated in cross country for only two years. He had a powerful body with a solid barrel chest, not your typical distance runner. Steve grew up on a country farmstead, baling acres of hay on hot Minnesota summer days.

Harrington completed medical school, got married and moved to Duluth in June of 1977. He began a three-year physician residency program that summer.

On Saturday, June 25, Steve walked two blocks downhill from his new home in the Lester Park neighborhood to watch Garry Bjorklund run in his first marathon.

The race inspired Steve and he began training for the 1978 Grandma's. He purchased a pair of New Balance running shoes from me at my store, The Running Shop.

Steve, a tireless worker, was not afraid to do year-round training. He ran in 1978 and finished 189th with a first marathon time of 3:09:04.

Steve loved the marathon distance. It was an athletic challenge he craved, although he disliked running on the snow packed, icy roads that Northern Minnesota produced five months of the year.

He soon found a new love – cross country skiing. With a strong upper body and the ability to learn proper technique, he found success with the sport.

Steve explained, "I excelled at skiing and I learned if you wanted to take it to the next level, you must have a solid running program in the off season."

Steve excelled all right. He was capable of skiing 55 kilometers in the 2:20 range, not far behind Olympic class athletes. In 1981 and 1982, he won the American Birkebeiner citizen race in Cable, Wisconsin. His victories earned all-expense-paid trips to the Norwegian Birkebeiner in Lillehammer. Skiing through the mountain ranges of Norway was a dream come true for Steve.

In 1986, Grandma's Marathon received a blessing when Steve agreed to become the medical director of our race. He had a clear understanding of the determination and drive of athletes. He knew runners were capable of amazing feats no matter the challenges they had on the racecourse.

Steve's philosophy coincided with mine. Let's plan for all possible weather conditions and develop every safety protocol necessary. The highest priority was to orchestrate a safe race for every runner.

Steve took an ethical approach to his planning with an understanding of the science of the sport.

Grandma's Marathon starting line in 1985.

Our mutual goal was always to ensure the race was held. Steve understood the obligations we had to the thousands of runners who came from all over the world. The policy we developed for cancelling Grandma's would need the approval of two of three people – Medical Director, Executive Director and Chairperson of the Board. This lifted the burden off of one person making the difficult decision to cancel.

Steve excelled with his leadership skills, guiding us in developing an exceptional medical tent at the finish. He created the necessary policies and procedures for our 400-person medical team.

Portable defibrillators were added at each mile on the racecourse. All 15 water stations were equipped with communications and first aid. Four medical tents were placed along the course that also served as dropout locations.

Steve followed the American College of Sports Medicine recommendations on the implementation of a warning system to alert runners on the course about the risk level in hot and humid conditions.

We ran safe races because of good planning and good safety protocols. The medical volunteers were well trained and highly qualified. All of our pre-planning efforts paid off and, as Steve tells it, we were also lucky at times.

In my eyes, Steve always looked at how we could run the race, not find ways to cancel it. For a race director, that was a blessing.

Steve ran numerous Grandma's Marathons and in 1985 finished 132nd in 2:41:43.

Steve has been married to his wife Ann for 44 years and they continue to live in their family home purchased in 1977. They have two daughters – Annalisa and Elizabeth. Both girls were extraordinary athletes and proficient in running and cross-country skiing at East High School, competing in numerous state championships. Both went on to ski at Dartmouth College and competed in the NCAA Championships.

Steve volunteered as a coach for cross country skiing at East High School for nine years. He was inducted into the Grandma's Marathon Hall of Fame in 2011 after serving as medical director for 25 years.

In 1996, Steve pursued a one-year sports medicine fellowship. He changed his career in mid-life to focus on his dream to work directly with athletes and help with injuries. Steve retired from medicine on December 31, 2015, just shy of his 65th birthday.

CHAPTER 22

The Diamond Pendant

Janis Klecker described 1987 and 1988 as two of her most important years in building a foundation for international competition. Janis was training at a high level, loved to compete and enjoyed vying for control in her races. Janis never backed down from her rivals.

She passed her regional dental board exams on June 15, 1987, at the age of 26, only five days before the United States Women's National Marathon Championships held in Duluth. Many of the top 100 American women would be traveling to Grandma's Marathon. It would be competitive, with prize money to the top 18 finishers.

On the morning of the race, Saturday, June 20, temperatures were warming rapidly. There were sunny skies with a light lake breeze and a starting temperature in the high 60s. The conditions were not favorable for the 4,700 starters.

The women's championship race ended up between Janice Ettle and Janis Klecker, the top two Minnesota entrants.

Klecker was quoted at the post-race media conference saying, "I could see Janice at the end and she couldn't see me, so I felt I had the advantage." Janis' form was flawless in capturing the National title, defeating Ettle by nine seconds.

Her victory (2:36:12) earned her $10,000 and a one-carat solitaire diamond pendant worth $3,500. To this day, Janis never takes off her most cherished marathon prize. The necklace was a special gift and reminds her of winning her first National Marathon Championship in her home state.

Klecker, Ettle, and Martha White, who placed third, earned spots to represent the United States in the 1987 Tokyo

International Marathon. It was a pivotal moment in Janis' life, becoming a dentist and winning a marathon in the same week.

Janis ran more than 50 marathons in her career, and qualified for five U.S. Olympic Marathon Trials. It all started in the summer of 1979 at age 19, taking her first serious strides as a runner. A few months later, she registered for the City of the Lakes Marathon in Minneapolis. Although young and inexperienced, she broke three hours, finishing in 2:58:32. An excellent start.

Janis was in top form in 1991, winning the Twin Cities Marathon in 2:30:31. Less than four months later, on January 26, 1992, she'd take part in the U.S. Women's Olympic Marathon Trials in Houston. There were 118 qualifiers, with 89 starters.

Janis Klecker wins the 1987 Grandma's Marathon in 2:36:12, the year Grandma's hosted the Women's National Championship Race. Klecker would go on to make the 1992 Olympic Marathon team and compete in Barcelona.

In the lead pack, at the mile 16 water station, Janis slipped and fell on the wet pavement. Pulitzer prize writer, Julie Cart, reporting for the Los Angeles Times described the fall.

"(Cathy) O'Brien led much of the marathon, but when Klecker fell on the slippery roadway, O'Brien ran back and helped Klecker to her feet." O'Brien showed compassion and humility. "In the last mile, Klecker passed O'Brien and turned one last corner to the finish. Klecker, who's face had been impassive the entire race, broke into a wide smile. She began to cry softly as she crossed the finish line and clasped her hands above her head. Klecker runs while holding her elbow away from her body at a sharp angle. No matter how odd it looks, it was effective. Klecker said the victory was like an answered prayer."

This was Janis's second National Marathon Championship victory.

* * *

The Women's Olympic Marathon in Barcelona, Spain, was on August 1, 1992. The starting time was 6:30 p.m. Forty-seven participants from 31 countries would run in the early evening hours in the second largest city in Spain. The second half of the course weaved through narrow streets with the buildings reflecting the heat from the warming blacktop.

The starting line temperature was 86 degrees with 60 percent humidity. It was a dangerous day to run the most prestigious marathon in the world, which only occurs every four years.

Janis stated, "I would rather run at 6:30 a.m. I wasn't trained properly for racing at this time of day. I tried to adjust, but it didn't work out for me. I remember how polluted the air was, the smog seemed to follow us throughout the course. The last two miles were uphill and the heat and humidity took its toll on many of the runners, including me."

American team:

- Cathy O'Brien – 10th Place – 2:39:42
- Francie Larrieu-Smith – 12th Place – 2:41:09
- Janis Klecker – 21st Place – 2:47:17

* * *

On September 22, 1991, in Syracuse, New York, Janis also won the Women's U.S. National 5K Championships, and was a past American 50K record holder with a time of 3:13:51.

Janis and Barney Klecker have six children – Mary, John, Sarah, Joe, Elizabeth (Bit) and James. The new love of their life is their first grandchild, Norman, who is named after Janis's Father.

Janis Klecker's Personal Record Times

- Mile – 4:51
- 5,000 Meters – 15:57
- 5 Miles – 25:50
- 10,000 Meters – 31:44
- Half Marathon – 1:10:41
- Marathon – 2:30:12
- 50 Kilometers – 3:13:51

CHAPTER 23

Doug Kurtis – A Legend

April 15, 1974, was a cool day in Boston with temperatures reaching 63 degrees - ideal running conditions for anyone taking the challenge of going 26.2 miles. Doug Kurtis of East Lansing, Michigan, was there on that beautiful spring day to attempt his first marathon. He did not have a qualifying time to gain entry into the race, but this didn't bother him. He simply made one up when he registered – he faked it.

The Boston Marathon, like most marathons during this era, was much less organized. No one from the Boston Athletic Association checked his registration information. Doug recalls there weren't even official water stations on the course.

Doug was an experienced runner, but a non-scholarship athlete who competed in cross country at Michigan State University for two years. In 1970 and 1971, Doug and his teammates were the Big Ten champions, with Doug being the team's seventh best runner.

Doug was undertrained for the marathon, averaging only 35 miles a week. At the start of the race in Hopkinton, Massachusetts, Doug was weaving through the masses, attempting to get as close as possible to the elite runners in the front row.

There were 1,951 registered runners, with only 46 women entered. Shortly after the starting gun fired, during the early downhill portions of the race, Doug found himself in trouble. His feet were developing blisters. He wore socks that crimped in his shoes. This was a huge mistake for any rookie or experienced marathoner. He was desperate, but certainly not willing to drop out. As he painfully continued along the course, Doug spotted a drug store near the 10-mile mark.

With his shoes in his hands, he left the racecourse and convinced the store clerk to give him a pair of Dr. Scholl's inserts so he could finish. Doug was grateful for the kindness, but now found himself another ten minutes behind.

Doug finished 247th with a time of 2:47:10, just one second ahead of Michiko "Miki" Gorman, the women's champion. Miki, 38, weighed just 89 pounds. She was shy and quiet, and mostly kept to herself, but was a fierce competitor, who outran her closest female competitor by almost six minutes.

Doug could be seen in the Boston papers the next morning in the photos of Gorman's final strides to victory.

Neil Cusak from Limerick, Ireland, studying at East Tennessee University, was the overall champion, finishing in 2:13:39. It was the third-fastest marathon in Boston history.

* * *

Very few runners across the globe have logged more miles than Doug Kurtis. In 53 years as an active runner, Doug has journeyed over 150,000 miles on the roads, trails and tracks in cities throughout the world. This is equivalent to almost 54 times from coast to coast of the U.S.

Doug's duration as a long-distance runner can be described as impressive, monumental and spectacular.

Doug's peers and the media regard him as one of the toughest and most consistent marathon runners in the world. From 1980 to 1995, he averaged 95 miles per week. His accomplishments are many, including 40 marathon victories, with 11 more as a master runner. His personal best time is 2:13:34, but even more impressive was his one-time world record of 76 sub-2:20 marathons.

Doug proclaims his longevity secret was simple. He loved to run, had no lifetime injuries and had the knack of recovering quickly after a race or hard workout.

As time has passed for all of us, Doug, now 68 years old, has broken three hours in the marathon 200 times, and qualified for the U.S. Olympic Marathon Trials five times.

Doug's Grandma's Marathon journey began in 1988 as an invited runner. He finished seventh that day in 2:23:55.

This is the same year Doug and I started a special friendship. I always loved Doug's energy. It was infectious. His personality is strong, but well disposed. Doug has always been friendly to the community members in Duluth. He truly enjoys talking to anyone who is willing to chat. Doug has endeared himself to our volunteers, marathon staff and each and every sponsor.

In 1989, Doug returned to Duluth and flew across the finish line with his arms raised high and his chest puffed out, breaking the tape in style. He ran a 2:16:37. Everyone at the finish enthusiastically celebrated his victory, and the photo of him crossing the finish line is one of the best in Grandma's Marathon history.

Doug enjoyed wearing his signature black cowboy hat during the award ceremony. He played up to the large crowds who were rocking in the Big Top Tent.

Doug ran Grandma's Marathon nine consecutive years from 1988 through 1996. He had two overall wins and five masters titles. He also participated in Grandma's in 2008, 2010, 2011 and 2013.

After his last Grandma's Marathon, Doug continued to be an important part of our events. He has been a guest speaker, a spokesperson to the media, a race announcer and has guided many course tours for runners each year.

Doug Kurtis flies through the finish ribbon in 1989 for this first Grandma's Marathon win.

Duluth has adopted Doug as one of our own. He is a true ambassador and has never been shy about proclaiming Grandma's as his favorite marathon.

In 1998, Doug called me and explained that he was being inducted into the Road Runners Club of America (RRCA) Hall of Fame on the same weekend as Grandma's. My quick response was, "You are going to the induction ceremony. It is a huge honor that rarely comes to anyone. There will be plenty more Grandma's Marathons." This was the only Grandma's Marathon weekend Doug missed since 1988.

Doug now lives in Asheville, North Carolina, with his wife, Ann. They enjoy hiking on local trails and spending time with friends.

Doug was inducted into the Grandma's Marathon Hall of Fame in 1999 alongside Olympic Bronze Medalist, Lorraine Moller.

Doug's Grandma's Marathon Times:

1988	7th Place	2:23:55
1989	1st Place	2:16:37
1990	2nd Place	2:18:37
1991	6th Place	2:17:59
1992	17th Place	2:23:47*
1993	1st Place	2:16:38*
1994	3rd Place	2:19:46*
1995	45th Place	2:27:41*
1996	15th Place	2:27:26*

**First place masters division*

CHAPTER 24

A Miracle at Grandma's

In 1990, I was successful in bringing the United States Women's National Marathon Championships back to Duluth in conjunction with Grandma's. Many of the best U.S. women distance runners would once again be traveling to Northern Minnesota to compete. The total prize money was $40,750. The total championship budget was $145,750.

Showcasing our beautiful city to runners from all over the nation and the world remained a priority for me. The financial investments became a significant part of our annual budget.

It was crucial to find additional sponsors to bring revenue to our nonprofit organization. I had to justify increased expenses to our 17-person board of directors. I informed them monthly about every detail of the race management and elite runner recruitment for the championships.

Since 1987, we were building a small cash reserve in our bank account. My philosophy was to invest one-half of each year's surplus for race improvements. The other half would be saved for unexpected financial emergencies. My goal was to eventually have one full year's budget in reserve in case we ever had to cancel the race.

* * *

1990 began with a personal heartbreak as my close friend, running mentor, and high school classmate, Ricky Brown, 36, died January 26 from a hard-fought battle with hemolytic anemia. It took months for me to accept his death. My grieving for him never seemed to end. I was functioning, but not at the level I needed to be.

At Ricky's funeral I was in tears and my friends who attended encouraged me to get control of my emotions.

Ricky Brown deserves much credit for helping the North Shore Striders start a marathon in Duluth. He always gave 100 percent effort in everything he tried. He was a once-in-a-lifetime friend, and I still think about him often.

* * *

On Friday, June 22, 1990, during the pre-race media conference, elite runner Jane Welzel told the heartbreaking story about her 1984 vacation in New Zealand. Jane described how she lost control of the car she was driving on a secluded dirt road. The car skidded off a hillside, rolling over three times and killing a cow before coming to a rest.

Jane, 35, a native of Hopkinton, Massachusetts, with her deep Bostonian accent, reflected on fracturing nine vertebrae in her neck and was in traction for two months, followed by a full body cast for another two. She barely escaped death.

This was obviously not a humorous story, but the way she told it, she could have easily been in Las Vegas doing a stand-up comedy act. The reporters were stunned by her story, but laughing at the same time. Jane became a media favorite for the race the next day.

* * *

Jane's marathon career began April 21, 1975, during the 79th Boston Marathon. She was 19 years old, a college sophomore attending the University of Massachusetts Amherst. During this era there were no organized women's track or cross-country programs at the university.

Jane loved to run and it seemed likely that she would participate in her hometown marathon. In her eyes, it wasn't a big deal; she just wanted to run 26.2 miles to downtown Boston.

Jane walked to the starting line from her nearby family home, not knowing she needed to officially register and obtain a race number. Jane, however, blended in with the other 2,400 participants.

There were 28 official women finishers that afternoon, but Jane wasn't one of them. She was disqualified as she crossed the finish line with a time of 3:35, because she hadn't officially entered.

It was a challenging, but exhilarating experience for her. She knew running marathons would become an important part of her life. After that first race, Jane went on to win the 1983 Philadelphia Marathon and finished 14th in the 1984 U.S. Olympic Marathon Trials with a time of 2:35:53.

* * *

In the November 1990 issue of *Running Times Magazine* an article written by Lark Farmer titled "A Miracle at Grandma's" described Jane's comeback from years of recovery and disappointments.

"When I started racing again, I was getting beat by everybody under the sun," recalled Jane, who had moved to Fort Collins, Colorado "But I couldn't stop. I just love to run." By 1989 she was well enough to finish fourth in the Twin Cities Marathon. Her comeback eventually led her to Duluth, where she stood among 4,424 starters.

At the sound of the gun, Jane set out with front-runner, Janis Klecker. The temperatures were quickly rising and at the

8 a.m. start it was already 68 degrees with clear, deep blue skies. Janis was wearing number one and Jane had number 4.

"I went out with her for the first mile, and by my watch it was 5:37," Jane recalled. "I felt a little uncomfortable and I thought, if she can keep this up, she deserves the win, and I eased off five or six seconds per mile."

Janis pulled steadily away during the first 10K. After a few more miles, however, the gap began narrowing between Janis and Jane. The temperature was in the low 70s by the time Janis reached the halfway mark in 1:15:10.

Jane caught Janis in the 14th mile and forged ahead.

A story titled "From Tragedy to Triumph" written by Jim Muff of the Duluth News Tribune in the Sunday paper explained that Jane's training before the championships included runs in 80-degree weather and high altitude in the Rocky Mountains. This came in handy late in the race. While her challengers were wilting, she attacked the three-mile stretch from Lester River to Lemon Drop Hill.

"When I got to 22-miles I told myself I was going to be excited, I was going to feel good, and I was going to keep going. Once I got to the top of the hill, I was cruising. I was confident and in control the whole way," said Welzel

"On paper I wasn't the one to win this race, but I learned to never count myself out of anything."

Jane broke the finish line tape and was handed a dozen red roses, her eyes partially closed with a huge smile of relief and joy. She ran 2:33:25 and earned $10,000. She was the best runner in the country on that warm day in Duluth.

Jane Welzel wins the 1990 Women's National Championship title in Duluth (2:33:25).

1990 U.S. Women's Championships			
1st place	Jane Welzel	2:33:25	$10,000
2nd place	Deborah Raunig	2:34:34	$7,000
3rd place	Gordon Block	2:35:48	$6,000
4th place	Janis Klecker	2:40:08	$4,000
5th place	Janice Ettle	2:40:21	$3,000

* * *

In 1992, Jane, 37, returned to Grandma's. A post-race article titled "No Plain Jane" written by Bruce Bennett from the Duluth News Tribune detailed how Jane caught the leader, Elena Semenova, at mile 18. Jane finally pulled ahead of the Ukranian somewhere after Lemon Drop Hill.

"I knew as long as I could maintain the pace I was doing, that nobody would come from behind and pass me," Jane said.

The weather was perfect that day with cool temps and a slight tailwind. Jane ran a personal best time of 2:33:01. She ran 1:16:30 in the first half and 1:16:31 the second half.

Bennett described Jane's beaming smile as she basked in the glory of a second Grandma's victory. "I told myself I'd done this before. I just had to keep going 'til the end. Everything went perfect for me. It was just one of those days that you pray for. Just ideal for me."

* * *

During the first week of December 1992, we brought Jane to the USA Track and Field (USATF) national meeting in Louisville, Kentucky, to be a part of our presentation team. We were bidding for the 1994 Women's National Marathon Championships. Jane was well respected by the national committee and I knew she would help us seal the deal to host a third championships.

On the third day of the conference, we received a unanimous vote. The championships were returning to Duluth, thanks in large part to the advocating Jane did on our behalf.

* * *

On August 31, 2014, at the age of 59, Jane died of pancreatic cancer in Fort Collins, Colorado.

Jane was a brave and lighthearted woman who touched the hearts of so many. She was a pioneer in the development of women's running in the United States. She only wanted people to be happy and enjoy the sport.

Jane was one of a few women to participate in five U.S. Women's Olympic Marathon Trials – 1984, 1988, 1992, 1996 and 2000.

The running community mourned her passing. I still remember her closed eyes and her smile of pure joy as she crossed the finish line at Grandma's.

CHAPTER 25

The Foundation

The creation of the Young Athletes Foundation (YAF) in 1990 remains one of the most significant community investments Grandma's Marathon has ever made. To this date, the YAF has contributed $1.2 million to youth athletic programs in five northern Minnesota and northwestern Wisconsin counties.

The mission of the foundation is to support and help build a strong community by providing a pathway for opportunities to youth through their involvement in sports.

The first program under the Young Athletes Foundation was a free race series for children ages 14 and younger called Wednesday Night at the Races. The races are held at parks and local tracks for six consecutive weeks during the summer. Every Wednesday night hundreds of children line up at the starting line waiting to run and receive a colorful ribbon at the finish line. Children receive T-shirts at the last race of the season and are treated with a picnic for the whole family. To date, approximately 50,000 children have participated in the races.

With the establishment of the foundation and the success of Wednesday Night at the Races, the YAF has expanded its community outreach through the following programs:

- Saturday Morning at the Races - A winter running series for kids held on the indoor tracks at the University of Minnesota Duluth, College of St. Scholastica and University of Wisconsin Superior.
- Running Shoe Program – More than 4,500 pairs of running shoes have been provided to area high school track and cross-country athletes in need.

- Grant Program – Thousands of dollars are given to youth athletic and recreation programs each year for equipment and financial needs.
- Eleanor Rynda Cross Country Scholarship - $1,200 is given annually to one female and one male UMD cross country runner.

Proceeds taken in from the Saint Fennessy 4K, Fitger's 5K, Park Point 5-Miler, Minnesota Mile and North End Nightmare 5K help fund these programs.

Back when the YAF began, we simply wanted to play a role in helping the up-and-coming runners and athletes in our area, and it fit the mission of Grandma's Marathon nicely. What we didn't know was how important the foundation would become and the impact it would have on the lives of so many youth.

Wednesday Night at the Races

CHAPTER 26

The Garry Bjorklund Half Marathon

When Grandma's Marathon began in 1977, it was a significant moment in the promotion of long distance running in Minnesota. It became a catalyst for people to set a goal, do some training and run 26.2 miles. Individuals were losing weight and improving their fitness level tenfold.

In 1991, the announcement to add a half marathon to race day became one of the most important decisions made by our organization. It played a monumental role in the beginning of a new local and regional running boom.

Anyone with moderate training and in good health could now feasibly run a race during Grandma's Marathon weekend and experience one of the Midwest's premier sporting events. The increased number of people jogging on the streets of Duluth after our announcement made it clear that we were on to something big.

Adding a half marathon had been in the back of my mind for many years. It was becoming difficult to watch some of the runners in the back of the marathon pack struggling to reach the finish line. The medical tents were swelling with runners and in 1990, with balmy temperatures, it was apparent we needed to do something different the following year.

Don Wicklund, a board member of Grandma's Marathon, and I took the initiative to design the plan for an appropriate half marathon starting area. The access roads from the expressway to the racecourse on the Scenic Highway were the perfect solution for transporting runners to the start. We even had a back road that joined the course just in front of the proposed starting line.

It was a relief that getting runners to the starting line would not be an obstacle. With a visual plan to stage a half marathon in

1991, Wicklund and I received full support from the board. We never dreamed that the plans we created would make it possible for us to eventually host six national half marathon championships.

I started planning the race details immediately and in the following months the necessary supplies and equipment were ordered. The course was measured and certified. The volunteers were recruited and now we just needed to find some runners.

We decided to limit the field to 1,500 participants. The entry fee was $20. Our marketing strategy was simple. We would host an on-site registration party in the upper level of Grandma's Sports Garden.

When the doors opened for the party, we were in total disbelief. There was a long line winding through the restaurant below, out the front door and down the block, ending at the foot of the Aerial Lift Bridge. Hours later we had collected $30,000 in cash and had 1,500 runners registered.

* * *

Adding another race was challenging in many ways, but at the same time it was exhilarating. We were doing the right thing by offering an alternative to the marathon. Our main objective was to get runners into the race that suited them best.

In 1991, few established marathons were adding races to their line-up. It was seen as a unique step for a race organization to take. I am not sure if we were the first marathon in the United States to do this, but we were definitely one of the first.

I always looked at myself as a purest in the sport, but almost immediately I started to receive criticism. Many so-called running experts who lived 150 miles south of Duluth in the Twin Cities were shocked. Letters and telephone calls were coming in daily with all of the same theme: "Great job on ruining Grandma's Marathon, Keenan." My peers felt Grandma's Marathon would soon cease to exist due to the addition of the half marathon.

Of course, in my typical way, I ignored them. We were already locked in and committed 100 percent to promoting a half marathon in Duluth which was named after a Twin Ports running legend, Garry Bjorklund.

Our statement to the naysayers was: Damn the torpedoes - full speed ahead!

Today almost every marathon organization has added a half marathon. Most of them have done so out of financial necessity.

The Twin Cities Marathon followed suit eight years later by adding a ten-mile race to their weekend events.

CHAPTER 27

Six Victories – Six Watches

With a late surge and leaning as far forward as he possibly could, Ryan Meissen, 23, from Hudson, Wisconsin, broke the finish tape for the Garry Bjorklund Half Marathon and defended his 2000 title (1:08:09). His effort earned him a personal best time and a course record by two seconds with a time of 1:06:10.

In the Sunday, June 17, 2001, edition of the Duluth News Tribune, staff writer, Irv Mossberger quoted the winner:

"I told a few friends of mine that I was going to set the record, so I wanted to go out and actually do it and not just talk about it. I looked up at the clock and it was 1:05:55. I knew it was going to be close, so I gave it everything I had."

Kelly Keeler, 39, from Bloomington, Minnesota, won the women's division of the Garry Bjorklund Half Marathon in 1:15:48, outlasting Janet Robertz of Shorewood, Minnesota, by 22 seconds. This was Keeler's third victory in Duluth, also winning the half marathon in 1998 and 2000. She received three Citizen watches for her wins.

* * *

Ryan Meissen had a humble beginning as a high school runner in Hudson. After graduation, he attended the University of Wisconsin-Whitewater from 1996 to 2000 and became a four-time cross-country NCAA Division III championship qualifier. In 1999, he was honored with All-American status, finishing 14th at nationals.

Ryan's love of the North Shore of Lake Superior started in 1994 when he was 16, running his first marathon at Grandma's.

The race became a struggle that day and he was unaware that runners could actually drop out.

He overcame many difficulties during the 26.2 miles, mentally and physically, and proved to himself he had strength of character and perseverance. Ryan finished in 3:26.

In 1995, Ryan returned to Grandma's Marathon better prepared and with more confidence. It was a good June day for him. He improved his time by 40 minutes, finishing in 2:46:50.

The following year, now 18, Ryan signed up for the Garry Bjorklund Half Marathon and finished 14th in 1:12:28. In 1997, Meissen finished the half marathon in 13th place in 1:13:22.

Ryan was rapidly becoming recognized as a Midwest elite runner and in 1999 won the Garry Bjorklund Half Marathon on his third try. His hard work and determination were paying off – he ran to victory in 1:08:14. During the award ceremony, Meissen received a Citizen watch for winning.

It was a gripping race to the finish. Ryan's mindset was, "I'm going to win this race no matter what." The race started with early morning fog enveloping the undulating roadway. The competition was strong, and the last three miles of the race was between Ryan and John Campbell of New Zealand. Ryan had absolutely no idea who this older guy was, but he was running fast.

A couple of months after the race, back home in Hudson, Ryan finally figured it out. It was John Campbell, 5-foot-8 and 126 pounds, born in New Zealand in February of 1949. He was a former milkman, shopkeeper and fisherman.

In 1990, John went undefeated as a master runner in 22 high profile races. He set master world records at four miles (18:31), 10K (29:04), 10 miles (47:55), 15K (45:10), half marathon (1:02:28) and finished fourth overall at the 1990 Boston Marathon in 2:11:04, the fastest marathon ever run by a runner over 40.

In 1988, at 39, John finished 12th in the marathon at the Summer Olympics in Seoul, Korea in 2:14:08.

John was one of the world's greatest runners and had earned more than $200,000 in prize money, when very few races in the world even offered money. Ryan Meissen was elated he won the race and beat Mr. Campbell.

John ran the 1998 Garry Bjorklund Half Marathon as well and finished third in 1:09:36. I was thrilled to invite John to Duluth and I had the opportunity to have some great conversations with him. He invited me to visit him in New Zealand. Unfortunately, I never made the trip.

* * *

In 2002, Ryan Meissen was once again ready to take on the half marathon. At the starting line, I could see a typical June thunderstorm stirring and heading up the North Shore. The sky was darkening, the wind was picking up directly out of the west, and you could smell rain in the air.

Thousands of runners were lined up and ready to go. I was giving my final instructions to the elite runners, explaining I had no choice but to send them off into the approaching storm. It would be better to spread everyone along the course, versus having them bunched up at the start. Good luck.

I was driving in front of the runners with the backup timing crew and when we just passed mile 9, we were forced to stop because there was zero visibility. The rain seemed to be coming down sideways. On the radio we heard the finish line announcers scrambling off the metal scaffolding. Lightning was surrounding the area with a vengeance.

"It was really raining hard for about ten minutes. Water was pooling everywhere on the road," Meissen said. "Afterward there was only a light rain with perfect cool running temperatures. I felt great, just a little wet."

Ryan crushed his own course record by almost two minutes, with a time of 1:04:19. He won a fourth consecutive Garry Bjorklund Half Marathon and a fourth Citizen watch.

In 2003, Ryan finished 21st in Grandma's Marathon. In 2004 and 2005, he once again stood on top of the champion's podium for the Garry Bjorklund Half Marathon with his fifth and sixth wins – six victories and six watches.

Since Grandma's Marathon weekend often falls on Father's Day weekend, two of the watches were given as gifts to his dad. One of the watches was given to his son, Croix, and the other three he kept.

* * *

Ryan went on to finish the Garry Bjorklund Half Marathon in 3rd place in 2006, 7th place in 2007 and 9th place in 2008. He had run Grandma's Marathon three times and the Garry Bjorklund Half Marathon 12 times. It was a 15-year run in Duluth.

On Monday, July 2, 2007, in the "Running Minnesota" blog, Ryan was asked what his fondest running memory was, and replied, "Winning the Garry Bjorklund Half Marathon in 1999, and every Grandma's Marathon weekend adds to those memories."

The follow up question was, "What is your favorite race?" and Ryan replied, "The Garry Bjorklund Half Marathon. The town really opens up and embraces the event. Whether you have a good race or strived for something a little better, you leave Duluth feeling special to have been part of this event."

When Ryan was in high school, he always had a copy of Runner's World Magazine in his backpack, with Steve Prefontaine on the cover. Pre was one of Ryan's heroes and in many ways he imitated Pre's running philosophy.

"I always gave it my all. There wasn't anything left. I just wanted to run as hard as possible," Ryan said. Ryan has been an important part of Grandma's Marathon weekend, and I am grateful for his loyalty.

He lives in Mukwonago, Wisconsin, with his wife, Kara, and two children, Croix and Clair.

Ryan Meissen broke his own Garry Bjorklund Half Marathon record by almost two minutes (1:04:19). This was his fourth consecutive half marathon win.

CHAPTER 28

Happy Anniversary

He Spoke. They Listened.

Bringing Billy Mills to Grandma's Marathon to be a part of our 25th anniversary in 2001 was a dream of mine and a tribute to him. Mills surprised the world by winning a 10,000-meter track gold medal for the United States in the 1964 Olympic Games in Tokyo.

He was the featured speaker during our Friday afternoon program in the Big Top Tent. He spoke about tolerance and shared a message of hope, and how we as people can live together in peace. He reflected on his come-from-behind victory in the Olympics. The title of his talk was "The Winning Spirit."

Mills, a Native American distance runner and member of the Oglala Sioux Tribe from Pine Ridge, South Dakota, worked countless hours raising money for national charities. A Marine who had served our country for 30 years, Mills is one of the most sought-after motivational speakers in the nation.

In 2012, Billy Mills was awarded the Presidential Citizen Medal presented to him by President Barack Obama. It is the second highest civilian award in the United States, second only to the Presidential Medal of Freedom.

Billy Mills was the 2001 Grandma's Marathon featured speaker. Mills was the 10,000 meter gold medal winner in the 1964 Olympics.

* * *

The Medallion

The 25th anniversary of Grandma's Marathon was a special time for a lot of people. It was a huge milestone for those of us who were deeply invested in the event.

It wasn't always clear sailing though. Over the years, I personally needed to be firm on many decisions, as I believed they were for the betterment and growth of our events. I was never one to look for confrontation, but I certainly wasn't one who would run from it either.

Some may have misconstrued my intentions, but I can honestly say I worked every day to build consensus with all of our stakeholders. My goal was two-fold. First, I was going to build a business, with revenue being generated from every possible direction. Second, I took that revenue to strengthen every aspect of our organization, from our staffing needs to providing every race amenity possible for the runners.

We were going to guarantee a safe and fun event for all, no matter what the cost. It was always about building a race experience that would be remembered.

Grandma's Marathon was an important part of our country's fitness revolution. The excitement and energy that was inspired by the runners, volunteers, sponsors and media has had an everlasting impact on many communities.

In any profession, there are weaknesses and I certainly have had my fair share but finding sponsors to help defray our expenses wasn't one of them. I loved making deals and it really didn't matter if it was for $500 or $50,000. In many ways I was obsessed with saving the marathon money.

I was once told jokingly by a board member, "Scott, whatever you do, please don't get a funeral home as one of our sponsors." My reply was, "That is a good idea. I never thought of that."

In planning for our 25th anniversary, I decided we needed a permanent display at the finish line to commemorate the race. My idea was to place a granite medallion, 6-feet in diameter, in the sidewalk adjacent to the finish line. I was successful in getting the City of Duluth and Maurices Corporation to sponsor and fund the project.

The medallion reads, "A Great Race On A Great Lake. Canal Park – Duluth, MN. Since 1977."

A six-foot granite medallion was permanently installed in the sidewalk next to the Grandma's Marathon finish line in 2001.

On Sunday, June 10, 2001, Mark Stodghill was interviewing me for the Duluth News Tribune, and followed me to where the brick sidewalk was being prepared for the placement of the medallion. I was asked how I wanted to be remembered.

Stodghill wrote: *You could almost see the thought balloon form over his head, but he couldn't find the answer. He finally said, "The most important things to me are that my grandkids and my wife think I'm a good grandfather and husband."*

"That has nothing to do with the marathon," said Stodghill

"I know." Keenan replied and turned to walk back to his office. There was still much work to be done.

* * *

Thank you, Dad

My dad quit drinking by age 50 and it was a revival for his life and those close to him. He was a new man who began to enjoy life to its fullest.

Dad had many one-liners to make a point. He was fun to be around and after my mother passed away in April of 1993, at age 66, he purchased a small trailer in Casa Grande, Arizona. He would live there in the winter months, escaping the cold and icy weather of northern Minnesota.

It was a close-knit retirement community with the residents helping each other. Dad, still a jokester, once made a small cardboard sign with a string to drape over his neck. The sign read: "Will work for food". He was glad to help others with small painting projects – his reward was a cup of coffee and a cookie.

Back in Duluth, Dad started a small business. Actually, it was more of a hobby – Chet's Collectibles. He loved finding antiques at a good price and reselling them for a marginal profit.

I am sure he never made a dime. It wasn't about making money; it was about getting out of the house and meeting people. He would talk to anyone willing to chat.

In the first three or four years of Grandma's Marathon, Chester Keenan was my secretary. All phone calls and mail were directed to Mom and Dad's house. I think Dad really enjoyed answering my phone calls and taking messages.

I was moving from apartment to apartment every year at that time, so 1533 West Arrowhead Road was basically a post office box for Grandma's Marathon. It was the constant I needed.

Dad was in charge of driving the race sag wagon for the first few years and worked traffic control with his best friend, Buck McDonald, for decades. Both were stationed near the train overpass by Knife River, ensuring that portion of the racecourse would be safe.

One week after our 25th anniversary race, we hosted our traditional volunteer pizza buffet celebration banquet at Grandma's Sports Garden.

Early in 2001, we created the Award of Excellence, a special recognition for those who have provided years of dedication, commitment, and service to the development of Grandma's Marathon.

The first recipient was my dad for his endless support. The other award given that night was for the Volunteer of the Year. My dad's best friend, Buck, was acknowledged. It was an emotional night, one that I was very proud to be part of.

In 2001, Scott Keenan's dad, Chester Keenan, was the first recipient of the Award of Excellence, a special recognition award for those who have provided years of dedication, commitment, and service to the development of Grandma's Marathon.

* * *

The Kiss on the Cheek

I was a distant acquaintance of Amby Burfoot, having met him a few times during trips to the Boston Marathon. Burfoot was the 1968 Boston Marathon champion (2:22:17) and editor-in-chief at Runner's World Magazine. He was in the upper echelon of marathon celebrities and I wasn't even sure he knew my name.

Over the years, I made numerous attempts to enlist Runner's World as one of our sponsors. In their eyes, Grandma's probably didn't have the appeal of higher profile races on the east and west coasts.

In 1988, Burfoot was having difficulty getting an interview with one of Minnesota's elite marathon runners. While in Boston, I mentioned to him I would be glad to make a telephone call on his behalf. The magazine got its interview shortly afterward.

A month or so before our June 16, 2001 race, 13 years after I did that small favor for Burfoot, I received a call. He was sending a writer and photographer to Duluth to cover our 25th anniversary run.

I was surprised but honored at the same time. This was really a big deal for me and a marketing dream for Grandma's Marathon. We made the necessary arrangements for lodging and credentials for the magazine.

On Friday, June 15, in the early afternoon, Garry Bjorklund, Dick Beardsley, and I were asked to meet the magazine photographer upstairs on the outdoor deck at Grandma's Saloon & Deli. He wanted to take a few photos of us with the iconic Aerial Lift Bridge in the background. The setting was beautiful, and I am truly honored when I can be in the company of these running legends.

Garry Bjorklund (left) and Dick Beardsley (right) are excited to be in Duluth to help celebrate the 25th anniversary of Grandma's Marathon with Scott Keenan (middle).

As always, with my life, there is usually a twist that occurs. The photographer wanted a unique picture and asked us to get a little crazy. Bjorklund and I didn't quite understand what he meant, but Beardsley did and gave me a big kiss on my cheek. The photographer got his photo. Just for the record – I didn't kiss him back.

A few months after the race, Runner's World published a multi-page spread about our anniversary.

I'm not sure why Burfoot went to the expense of covering our race but, deep in my mind, I would like to think he remembered the small favor I did for him. No matter the reason, I was truly grateful for the coverage.

Mark Stodghill of the Duluth News Tribune, on Sunday, June 10, 2001, wrote an article headlined, "See Scott Run," in which he contacted Burfoot for comments on Grandma's Marathon. Stodghill wrote:

Straight-shooting Grandma's Marathon director, Scott Keenan, has worked tirelessly for a quarter-century to make sure the course is up to par.

Burfoot credits Keenan with building Grandma's into a race worthy of worldwide attention.

"As someone observing his race at a little bit of distance over the past 25 years, what impresses me is the way he developed an idea, turned it into a great race and burnished it into a jewel," Burfoot said. "Runners feel Duluth rolls out the red carpet for them. It has the organization that you expect from a great marathon, but more than that, it has small town friendliness, charm and scenic appeal along with a big-time "do things right" professional organization."

A quarter century was a big deal for Grandma's Marathon. It had been a prominent sporting event in northern Minnesota for many years. I was going to make sure everyone was aware of this milestone.

Runners from 49 states and 41 countries were represented. The marathon reached its capacity in just 14 days with 9,159 registrants, and another 4,837 were accepted in the half marathon. The William A. Irvin 5K had 1,208 registered. A total of 15,264 runners were invited to our party.

The formula for our success has been simple. It is all about our beautiful racecourse along the North Shore of Lake Superior, the energy of thousands of volunteers and finishing in Canal Park, where the celebration begins.

Dick Beardsley, age 45, wearing race number 5848 finished the marathon that year in 2:55:39, fulfilling his goal of breaking three hours. Beardsley was still wearing a mustache, albeit a little bit greyer, which became his signature look when he set the Grandma's course record in 1981.

Shortly after the halfway point, Beardsley began drafting off other runners, who were more than willing to assist the running celebrity. In an article in the Duluth News Tribune by Mark Emmert, Dick was quoted saying, "I got so emotional the last couple of miles. I was getting goose bumps on my goose bumps.

The emotion was going through the crowd like a wave. I was getting all choked up out there."

It was a celebration for Dick. He was still running 20 years after his life-changing race along the North Shore. It was Dick's way of saying thank you to all of his supporters while being part of Grandma's 25-year gala.

Dick Beardsley breaks three hours in 2001 as part of his celebration of Grandma's 25th anniversary.

Garry Bjorklund and his wife Rhonda celebrated the weekend as well by running the race that bears Garry's name. They finished together with smiles on their faces.

CHAPTER 29

A New Step Forward

In December of 2002, during the U.S. Track and Field National meetings in Indianapolis, Indiana, Grandma's Marathon was awarded the 2003 and 2004 USA Women's Half Marathon Championships. Previously Grandma's was awarded the 1987, 1990 and 1994 women's marathon championships, but this would be the first time hosting the half marathon championships.

The prize money was set at $25,750 per year, with additional incentive money available for sub-1:16 performances.

Ryan Lamppa, media director for USA Track and Field, was quoted saying, "The 2003 half marathon in Duluth on June 21, is the deepest field for a national championship road race outside of the Olympic Marathon Trials."

The top three finishers qualified for the world half marathon championships in Vilamoura, Portugal on October 4, 2003. The top 13 runners in the Duluth competition had run personal record times that were faster than the course record of 1:14:11, set by Lauren Park in 1995.

There were a record number of registered runners – 16,218 total – in all of our races:

- Grandma's Marathon – 9,578
- Garry Bjorklund Half Marathon – 5,368
- William A. Irvin 5K – 1,272

This was a huge weekend for tourism in Duluth, generating over $8 million for the local economy.

The three half marathon favorites were Colleen De Reuck, 39, of Boulder, Colorado, with a best half marathon time of 1:08:33; Christine Clifton, 30, of Kirkland, Washington, with a best of 1:10:37 and Jennifer Rhines, 28, of Ardmore, Pennsylvania, with a best of 1:11:55.

De Reuck, a native of South Africa and a naturalized U.S. citizen, would wear race number one. During the pre-race media conference, De Reuck downplayed the fact that she was favored to win, explaining that her 1:08 half marathon was run more than a decade earlier.

On race morning, De Reuck set a swift pace, which intimidated the others in the lead pack. It wasn't the strategy that De Reuck had planned. She preferred to run with a group, but felt strong and decided to go for it.

De Reuck crossed the finish line in Canal Park in 1:10:00, setting a Garry Bjorklund Half Marathon women's course record by four minutes and eleven seconds, and breaking the USA Half Marathon Championship record by one minute and one second.

De Reuck earned $8,000 on that perfect running day along the North Shore of Lake Superior.

Christine Clifton finished second in 1:11:31 and Jennifer Rhines was third in 1:11:59.

* * *

Fira Sultanova, 41, of Moscow, Russia, was excited to run Grandma's Marathon in 2003. She didn't see her age as a barrier of any kind. She came to Minnesota to win and set a course record. She also had her eyes set on breaking the women's masters world record held by England's Priscilla Welch of 2:26:51.

Unlike De Reuck, Sultanova didn't downplay her ambitions. Two months earlier she finished seventh in the Boston Marathon, with a time of 2:31:30. She easily won the masters division.

Her recovery from Boston's effort came quickly, and she was well- rested for Grandma's on June 21.

The race ended up being a one-woman show. Sultanova cruised the point-to-point course with confidence. The weather was perfect for fast times, and her half marathon split was 1:12:02. Sultanova was on a mission to prove to the world she was deserving of a world marathon ranking.

Sultanova broke the finish tape, with both arms raised, in 2:27:05, shattering Elena Makolova's 1999 Grandma's time of 2:29:12.

Sultanova achieved two of her goals but missed the world masters record by 14 seconds. She earned $34,750; the largest amount of money ever paid out at Grandma's Marathon. Her time marked the largest victory margin in race history – she won by six minutes and forty-eight seconds.

Elly Rono, 32, of Kenya won the 2002 Grandma's Marathon men's title in 2:10:57 and was the race favorite in 2003. His goal was to break Dick Beardsley's 1981 course record of 2:09:37. Rono wasn't bashful about telling everyone about his aspirations.

The weather was ideal for Rono's attempt. The temperature was 55 degrees at the 7:45 a.m. start. The race came down to the tall, lanky six-foot, two-inch Rono, and the five-foot, three inch Joseph Kamau of Kenya. After both finished their charge up Lemon Drop Hill near 22 miles, Rono's pace began to slow. Kamau took advantage and seized a dominating lead as he approached the brick-laid portion of the course entering downtown Duluth on Superior Street.

In 2002, Kamau ran Grandma's Marathon, but was frustrated with his effort and dropped out at mile 25, kitty corner from the Radisson Hotel where he was staying. This isn't what race directors like to see, but Kamau was now making amends and increasing his distance over Rono. Kamau finished in 2:11:22, beating race favorite Rono by more than two minutes.

* * *

On May 29, 2004, Deena Drossin Kastor, 31, of Mammoth Lakes, California, registered to compete in the USA Women's Half Marathon Championships during Grandma's Marathon weekend. There were 75 elite women from across the country entered in the June 19 race.

Kastor was my number one recruit, and getting her commitment was a celebrated moment for Grandma's Marathon. In the most general terms it was a gigantic leap forward for road racing for the state of Minnesota. For days, I was smiling from ear to ear.

Kastor was assigned race number one, and was the clear favorite for the national title.

Kastor's running resume' was impressive. She was ranked as one of the best women's distance runners in the world, and was an eight-time All-American collegiate athlete at the University of Arkansas. She had successfully converted her track racing career to the roads, and her focus was on the marathon. The half marathon championship was a final tune-up leading to the 2004 Olympic Marathon in Athens, Greece, on August 22, just two months later.

The championship was our vehicle for continuing to attract elite women runners to Duluth. Once again, our motive was simple: We were going to showcase our race and beautiful city to America's best athletes.

After the Friday afternoon media conference and the mandatory technical meeting for the championship participants, Deena Kastor asked me to explain the last portion of the course to her. My answer was, "Let me show you instead." We hopped into my truck and drove the last mile of the course, carefully going over every detail.

Kastor was planning to run fast Saturday morning. She not only wanted to win and be crowned national champion, she also wanted to break the course record set the year before by Colleen DeReuk, AND break Joan Benoit Samuelson's national record of 1:08:34.

DeReuk wasn't entered to defend her title, but Kastor was sure of her ability, no matter who was running. On April 13, 2003, she finished third at the London Marathon and set an American record in 2:21:16. She was also named the 2003 American female road racer of the year.

Kastor, born in February of 1973, finished in second place at the U.S. Women's Olympic Trials in Saint Louis, Missouri, on April 3, 2004. De Reuck finished first with a time of 2:28:35, Kastor recorded a 2:29:38 and Jen Rhines was third in 2:29:57.

The temperature was cool and hovering around 48 degrees for the early 6:15 a.m. start. The wind was brisk from the southwest and blowing between 10 to 12 miles per hour. It would be a challenging day, as the participants would face a headwind for twelve of the 13.1 miles.

Kastor planned an even pace strategy, running 5:15 per mile, for a time of 1:07 or 1:08. After the first mile it was apparent, she needed to go to plan B, and just focus on winning the race. She settled into a 5:20 per mile pace.

Sunday's Duluth News Tribune story by staff writer Jon Nowacki had a headline which said it all – "Kastor Wins In A Breeze".

Nowacki wrote, "Deena Kastor had a dominating Duluth performance during a brief stop on her way to the Athens Olympics in August. 'I still have plans for Athens down the line, so at Grandma's I just wanted to have a strong race. I think I did that. I felt good out there'," Kastor said.

Kastor had such a commanding lead during the race that she had time to look at real estate along London Road and contemplate purchasing a retirement home.

"It's been wonderful in Duluth," Deena said. "I saw two homes for sale that I really want. It was hard to miss those things. They were monsters – just gorgeous.

"It really wasn't that bad running alone. I can't emphasize enough how important the fans are along the route, and how grateful I am for them getting up so early to be there. They were amazing."

2004 U.S. National Half Marathon Championships:

1. Deena Kastor, Mammoth Lakes, California – 1:10:30 - $8,000
2. Susannah Beck, Yarmoth, Maine – 1:15:03 - $5,000
3. Cori Mooney, Boise, Idaho – 1:15:17 - $4,500
4. Rachel Kinsman, Archbold, Ohio – 1:15:20 - $3,500
5. Jenny Spangler, Lakevilla, Illinois – 1:15:29 - $4,000 (Jenny set a new masters course record with her time)

Deena Kastor took her race in Duluth seriously. She arrived on Tuesday before the race to make sure she was well rested and knew the racecourse. I put Deena and her husband, Andrew, up in a spacious room overlooking Lake Superior at Fitger's Inn. She was often seen shopping in the complex's stores.

If we'd only had better weather conditions, Deena could have easily set an American half marathon record that day. After the race, she quickly changed shoes and greeted the other elite runners as they crossed the finish line.

Deena was a class act in every possible way and had a broad smile as she enjoyed celebrating with the large crowd at the finish.

* * *

Going into the Olympics, Deena wanted to do what no American woman had done since Joan Benoit Samuelson won the first women's Olympic marathon in 1984. She wanted a medal.

Eighty-two women from 46 nations would start the marathon at the 2004 Summer Games of the XXVII Olympiad in Athens, Greece. The weather on August 22 was hot and humid and the temperature at the 6 p.m. start was expected to reach 100 degrees.

However, the weather gods ended up showing some compassion. Temps reached only 86 degrees with 50 percent humidity when the starting gun was fired. The extreme heat put the runners in danger and Kastor took a pedestrian approach for the first half of the race, running comfortably in 18th place. During the second half she gradually passed runners, one at a time.

The marathon followed the route Pheidippides took from Marathon to Athens in 490 BC. The race would finish at the Panathinaiko Stadium where the first modern Olympics were held.

As Kastor approached the stadium, she overtook the third place runner, and secured the bronze medal with a time of 2:27:20 – exactly one minute behind the gold medal winner.

Gold Medal – Mizuki Noguchi, Japan – 2:26:20
Silver Medal – Catherine Ndereba, Kenya – 2:26:32
Bronze Medal – Deena Kastor, USA – 2:27:20

This was a dream come true for Deena. She crossed the finish line with tears of joy and proved once again that she was one of the best runners in the world.

After the Olympics, Deena continued to run well, winning the 2005 Chicago Marathon in 2:21:25. In 2006, she won another of the World Major Marathons in London in 2:19:36, which still stands as an American marathon record.

Kastor's journey for a bronze medal in Athens went through Duluth – a day I will always remember.

CHAPTER 30

Special Edition – Speaks Loudly

Grandma's Marathon would be the second race to be honored with a special edition of Marathon & Beyond Magazine. The first to receive the honor was the Boston Marathon – titled Boston & Beyond, celebrating the race's 110th anniversary.

In June of 2005, Rich Benyo, editor of the magazine was on his biennial pilgrimage to Grandma's Marathon. During his stay, he talked in a general sense about the possibility of Grandma's being featured in the next special edition book.

My eyes couldn't have gotten any larger. My hand was extended quickly with Rich instinctively shaking it. I am sure he could see the twinkle in my eyes and my scheming grin, and was thinking, "What did I just do?"

On Monday, June 19, two days after Grandma's Marathon, I was driving Rich to Duluth International Airport following a lunch at Fitger's Brewhouse to recap the weekend. During the ride, I looked in the sky and predicted that a June thunderstorm was on its way and more than likely his flight would be delayed.

Rich was slightly puzzled by my prediction, but as we were arriving at the airport, the rain began. The flight was delayed, so Rich purchased the local paper and read Kevin Pates' interview with me about our plans for the next year's 30th anniversary. I explained that we would have a North Shore Striders Reunion and would be partnering with Marathon & Beyond to produce a special edition called "Grandma's Marathon & Beyond".

Rich slithered down his rigid plastic airport chair, muttering to himself that he would never shake my hand again. His thought was, "Boy they work fast up here in Duluth." Rich couldn't get out of town fast enough as he contemplated what just happened.

There were no attorneys needed, not even a contract. A firm handshake had sealed the deal.

* * *

Marathon & Beyond was a joint venture with Rich Benyo and Jan Seeley. They printed their first bi-monthly edition in 1996.

Grandma's Marathon & Beyond was a time-consuming, but wonderful, special project to be a part of. It was a priority for us to provide everything the magazine needed, and the staff of Grandma's Marathon was available to assist Rich and Jan in all aspects.

Rich and Jan wrote the following forward for the book:
Occasionally a marathon emerges that manages to do the impossible – to combine the best qualities of marathons that are so seemingly diverse that they have absolutely nothing in common. The closest combination of all the essentially positive elements of a marathon blended into one that we've been able to find is Grandma's Marathon.

This probably explains why Grandma's Marathon holds the distinction of earning the highest score of any marathon that Marathon & Beyond has ever reviewed – and there have been 57 marathons reviewed to date in the magazine's history. Grandma's score was 968 points out of a possible 1000.

* * *

The Leavitts lived across the street from my friends Roger and Dorothy Spencer on Columbus Avenue in Duluth. They were close neighborhood friends and members of the North Shore Striders.

At the 29th Grandma's Marathon, Catherine Leavitt-Olson, presented me with a replica North Shore Striders T-shirt. It was a tearful moment, which certainly brought memories of our old running club that was responsible for starting Grandma's Marathon in 1977.

My original club shirt, size medium, was long gone, and this moment was the driving force to organize the first North Shore Strider's reunion as part of the 30th anniversary.

We had more than 100 club members attend and the marathon provided shirts with names printed on the back. It was a historic gathering with a Friday evening social. Everyone received two VIP credentials for the weekend, and refreshments.

Each club member had the option to run one of our races for free. The most important part of the weekend was having the North Shore Striders inducted into the Grandma's Marathon Hall of Fame.

Thank you, Catherine Leavitt-Olson! Your inspiration will never be forgotten. You're a North Shore Strider forever!

Catherine Leavitt-Olson and Scott Keenan are proud members of the North Shore Striders.

* * *

The weather for Grandma's Marathon 2006 was less than ideal, with the temperature climbing to 78 degrees by noon. The warming southwest wind brought humid conditions, with almost an inch of rain pouring down about 3 p.m. as the final runners were approaching the finish.

The medical team was stressed with patients, lightning was brightening the darkened sky, threatening to strike the metal posts on the large circus-type tents used to house the finish line medical operations and post-race party.

It was the second largest marathon field in our history, with 9,758 registered runners. All together our weekend races topped 17,000 entries. The cost of organizing the race in 2006 was $1,871,755 – 3,120 times the price of organizing our inaugural race thirty years earlier.

Grandma's Marathon was now in the big leagues of United States marathons and had become a driving force in American running.

The North Shore Striders help celebrate the 30th Anniversary of Grandma's Marathon in 2006

CHAPTER 31

A Dream Come True

Her right arm was held high, clearly showing the muscle definition of her upper torso. Kara Goucher's mouth was wide open, yelling with the joy of victory. You could feel her emotions and see the relief on her face in winning the USA National Half Marathon Championships in her hometown.

A 2012 story by Rachel Blount of the Minneapolis Star Tribune was headlined, "Goucher says Victory is a 'Dream Come True'". It described the night before the championships when Kara looked out the window of her room at Fitger's Inn and took in the view. "It was the best feeling in the world," said the Duluth native. "I am so proud to be from here."

Blount noted that Duluthians are just as proud of her, which helped power her to victory in an emotional return to where her career began. Goucher, 33, won the U.S. title in a women's course record 1:09:46.

Goucher said "The race felt like a high school reunion," with people from her past calling out to her along the route.

As Kara crossed the finish line, spectators who lined up four-deep along Canal Park Drive delivered a rousing ovation. Among them were her teary-eyed grandparents, her mother and other relatives who waited 16 years to see her run again in her hometown.

Goucher was further quoted, "I've never gotten goose bumps like I got today coming down Superior Street. I couldn't ask for anything more."

In a Duluth News Tribune article on Sunday, June 17, 2012, headlined "Hometown Hero Delivers", written by Rick Weegman, a photo by Clint Austin showed Goucher holding her baby son, Colt, in one arm and raising the American flag with the other. Goucher was smiling and you could just tell how proud she was.

Weegman wrote, "Near the finish line, a fist-pumping Kara Goucher finally was able to show what returning to Duluth meant to her. Goucher will run the marathon at this year's summer Olympics in London." Goucher explained, "Every elite athlete dreams big dreams when they are growing up, and for me to come here on my way to the Olympics, I couldn't have asked for anything more."

Weegman continued, "It's a long time removed from when Goucher used to hand out water to runners on London Road, and wonder why anyone would ever run 26.2 miles. "I never thought I'd run the marathon; I thought they were crazy," she said. "A lot of my friends would run the half marathon, which was just starting, and I thought they were crazy."

"The community has embraced me forever – when I started running when I was 12, almost 22 years ago – and they've been there for me through it all. For me to come back and do this, it's the best way I can thank them."

The first night Kara arrived in Duluth for the half marathon championships she was elated to go for a run-on London Road along the race course. It brought good memories to her and there was no doubt in her mind she would do everything in her power to win.

"Secretly, I wanted to set a new course record and I never felt that way before in a race," Goucher said. "My coach, Jerry Schumacher, only wanted me to run 5:25 per mile pace for the first nine-and-a-half miles. I was mad at him. I wanted to go faster, and I wanted to go earlier. This race was one of my most exciting and memorable races in my life. I love Duluth."

On that day, Kara felt she could have run a sub 1:09 half marathon but had to remember this was a training race for London.

Kara's mile splits were: 5:16, 5:20, 5:17, 5:25, 5:29, 5:21, 5:27, 5:22, 5:17, 5:17, 5:14, 5:11 and 5:03.

2012 USA National Half Marathon:

Women

1	Kara Goucher, Portland, Oregon	1:09:46
2	Maegan Krifchin, Long Island, New York	1:10:55
3	Michelle Frey, Minneapolis, Minnesota	1:11:45

Men

1	Abdi Abdirahman, Tucson, Arizona	1:02:46
2	Brett Gotcher, Flagstaff, Arizona	1:02:49
3	Ian Burrell, Tucson, Arizona	1:02:51

Kara Goucher wins the 2012 USA Half Marathon National Championship in her hometown of Duluth, Minnesota.

Kara earned $12,000 in prize money and $2,000 in incentive money. Abdi earned $12,000 in prize money and $1,250 in incentive money.

There was $77,500 in prize money for the top 12 women and men, and an additional $5,000 for the top three women and men 40 and over. A total of $82,000 was awarded.

Abdi Abdirahman was born in Somalia and became a United States citizen in 2000. He was a world-class track athlete who had run 27:16:99 for 10,000 meters. He represented his new country in the 2000 Olympics in Sydney, 2004 in Athens and 2008 in Beijing.

His journey to Grandma's Marathon started January 14, 2012, when he ran a 2:09:47 marathon and finished third at the U.S. Olympic Marathon Trials in Houston, Texas. He qualified for his fourth Olympic Games and his first at the marathon distance.

The men's Olympic Marathon would be August 12, 2012, in London. Both Abdirahman and Goucher earned $52,000 for third place finishes at the trials. They had the same plan, to run the U.S. Half Marathon Championships in Duluth as a tune up. They would train through it and not taper. Both had a goal to medal in the London Olympics.

The morning after the national championships in Duluth, Rick Weegman's story on Abdirahman was headlined "First Time In Duluth Is A Charm For Olympian". Weegman quoted Abdirahman, age 35, "I felt good. I'm in the middle of heavy training so I didn't rest for the race. My body wasn't well rested, but at the same time I came here to run well and do the best that I can. If I won, it would be a bonus."

"You don't want to come to a race and not give 110 percent. You don't want to cheat people on effort. At the same time, if you run well, you get rewarded."

Abdirahman defeated Brett Gotcher of Flagstaff, Arizona, by three seconds and Ian Burrell of Tucson, Arizona, by five seconds.

Abdirahman added, "The surface is the best that I've ever run on. The pavement is amazing. It's really one of the best road races I've been in. I love it. I have no regret coming here as it's been an amazing weekend. Plus winning doesn't hurt either."

* * *

On Monday, April 15, 2013, during the 117th Boston Marathon, 23,000 runners lined up in Hopkinton, Massachusetts to help celebrate the oldest marathon in the world. It is always held on Patriot's Day, a regional holiday honoring the colonists who fought for independence from Great Britain.

Kara Goucher loved attending the Boston Marathon. She loved the traditions of the race and was overwhelmed with the support she received running through the communities on the point-to-point course. In many ways it was similar to her hometown racecourse in Duluth.

It had the small-town feel that provided a sense of comfort to her. She knew she could run well, and was definitely at peace as she competed against the world's finest runners. This was Goucher's third Boston Marathon and, in 2011, she ran her personal best time of 2:24:52.

The temperature on race morning in 2013 was cool, with the high only reaching 53 degrees. The sun was partially blocked by low clouds.

The race was competitive with Rita Jeptoo of Kenya taking the women's olive branch winner's wreath in 2:26:25. Shalane Flanagan was the first U.S. finisher, fourth in 2:27:08 and Kara Goucher was the second American, sixth overall in 2:28:11.

Approximately two hours and fifty minutes after Goucher crossed the finish line, two homemade pressure cooker bombs detonated 12 seconds apart on Boylston Street near the finish of the race. Three spectators were killed, with another 264 injured.

Road racing as we knew it was changed forever.

Goucher had completed her media obligations after the race and headed back to her hotel room to rest and catch up with her family.

"I never heard anything like it when the first bomb exploded," Goucher said. "I ran to the window and opened it. Then the second bomb blew. I was really scared. I thought I was going to die."

Kara could see police rolling racks of guns out of their vehicles down on ground level. People everywhere on the street were running in a panic, and the television reports were beginning to tell the story of what had happened.

The elite runner celebration banquet at the host hotel was cancelled. Food was placed in a buffet style for the runners to help themselves. Kara, utterly exhausted and in despair, wore her pajamas to get her plate of food.

Kara and her family were, thankfully, heading back to Minnesota in the morning. The tragedy that struck in Boston would have an everlasting effect on her life. For the next three days she did nothing but watch television with hopes the attackers would be caught. She did everything she could not to cry.

* * *

Two months later, June 22, 2013, marked the second and last year of our contract with the United States Track and Field to host the men and women's National Half Marathon Championships. The extra responsibilities and workload was a challenge for the staff and volunteers.

We had to organize our Whipper Snapper Races for Kids and the William A. Irvin on Friday; and the Garry Bjorklund Half Marathon and Grandma's Marathon on Saturday morning. We now had six important events to host, with over 18,000 runners.

Our races were just seven weeks after the bombings in Boston. Major races across the country had security before, but because of the nightmare in New England, new strategies were needed.

Grandma's Marathon was one of the first major marathons in the country after the Boston bombing. There was deep concern about a possible attack at Grandma's. I started the conversation with the Duluth Police Department immediately. Meetings were scheduled with every law enforcement agency in the area and safety protocols were rewritten.

Grandma's Marathon was in the hands of Homeland Security, FBI, Coast Guard, Highway Patrol, St. Louis County Sheriff's Office and the Duluth Police Department.

The safety of the runners, volunteers and spectators was our highest priority. A police mobile command center was brought to the finish area and cameras were set up in locations around Canal Park. On race morning the police presence was increased tenfold throughout the racecourse and bomb-sniffing dogs were working overtime.

Many runners commented after the race that they were grateful for the high level of security. Police were everywhere.

In so many ways the fun of organizing races was now taken away. The new era of race directing was not appealing – did the Boston Marathon bombings play a role in my retirement? Yes, absolutely.

* * *

Kara Wheeler was six years old when Grandpa Calvin Haworth introduced her to a one-mile kids race in Hermantown, Minnesota. The event was part of the annual Summerfest celebration in the community on the western edge of Duluth. Kara was wearing a new pair of Keds sneakers.

Haworth, a lifelong runner, ran alongside Kara as the race started. Shortly after, Kara tripped and fell, skinning a knee.

Grandpa was greatly surprised by Kara's eagerness to continue and she eventually caught up to the other kids.

Kara's running career started that day, as she demonstrated strong fortitude and a refusal to quit.

At age eleven, Kara received her first pair of real running shoes, and she and her mom, Patty, entered the Mother's Day 5K Run in Duluth. This would be Kara's first 5K. After that, there was no stopping her. She fell in love with the sport and never looked back.

Kara was twelve when she joined cross-country at Woodland Middle School and quickly found a new love as part of an organized team.

East High School coach, Dick Skogg, recognized Kara's talent when she participated in the middle school division of the Swain Cross Country Invitational. Kara was invited to join the high school track team the following spring. She wholeheartedly accepted.

Kara's success came quickly and, as an eighth grader representing East, finished third in the 1991 Minnesota State High School Class AA Cross Country Meet. Carrie Tollefson, a future Olympian from Dawson, Minnesota, won the title.

Kara averaged only 30 training miles per week but didn't mind as she was improving every race and it fit her high school lifestyle. She was involved in other activities, including student government, orchestra, pep band, cross-country skiing, and summer soccer, while maintaining a solid GPA.

"I remember the team would go for a run and we would end up at Mount Royal Fine Foods buying donut holes. Coach Skogg didn't care. He was just upset that we didn't bring any back for him," Kara said.

Kara had many memorable experiences in high school, graduating in 1996. "The most important thing for me was to hang out with my friends. When I return to Duluth for a visit, we still get together."

Kara twice qualified for the Foot Locker Cross-Country Nationals and was a state champion in track and cross-country. Her personal best high school times:

1600 M – 5:00:92
3200 M – 10:48
5000 M (cross-country) – 17:48

Deciding on a college wasn't the easiest process for Kara. She finally made an oral commitment to Georgetown, a private university in Washington, DC.

Although she was out of eligible paid visits to schools, she still wanted to check out the University of Colorado in Boulder. Her mom purchased a plane ticket and Kara fell in love with the community. It gave her the same feeling of being in Duluth, with the weather being much better year-round.

Kara received an athletic scholarship for four years at Colorado, and then faced a difficult orientation to Division I running. The intensity was higher, and the mileage increased to over 70 miles per week.

"I was often injured, but coach Mark Wetmore taught me the necessary skills for running and racing at this level. My experience at Colorado was a good one," said Goucher.

In 2000, Kara became the NCAA Outdoor Track Champion at 3,000 and 5,000 meters. She followed that up in the fall with a win at the NCAA Cross-Country Championship.

She won the Honda Sports Award as the best collegiate cross-country runner in the nation in 2001 and graduated the same year from the University of Colorado with a degree in Psychology. The same year she married fellow distance runner and Colorado alum, Adam Goucher. In September 2010, the couple welcomed their son, Colt, into the world.

CHAPTER 32

Saying Good-bye

It was a fair-minded decision. I knew my retirement from Grandma's Marathon would happen sooner than most people predicted.

I had been contemplating retiring for three years but was afraid to act on it. My wife, Carrie, was the only person I was willing to share my feelings with. She knew I was under more and more stress each year. I wasn't very good hiding it from her. I was frequently irritable and not fun to be around. I regret those moments.

The race was taking a toll on me mentally and physically, and I was beginning to have concerns about my health. I didn't want to suffer a heart attack because of the self-induced pressure. It was becoming clear to me I needed to find a new chapter in my life.

To be honest, weather played a major factor in a decision to move on. As any outdoor event organizer knows, predicting the weather on event day is extremely stressful.

In 2013, it looked like we would have to cancel our Saturday races. The weather professionals agreed that a major thunderstorm would roll into the area in the early morning, just as the USA Half Marathon Championships would be starting. Thankfully, the storms went a few miles south of Duluth, and the conditions ended up being ideal. We were lucky yet again.

* * *

Of course, other factors played into my decision. Duluth, being a small market, made fundraising a challenge. I needed to spend two or three hours a day keeping our sponsors engaged and hoping to find new ones. I took pride in all of our partnerships and was able to secure more than 100 sponsorship agreements annually. Many became good friends, and many of them are still sponsors today.

Raising money is hard, and when I lost a sponsor, I took it personally. I felt in some way I didn't do my job. As time went on and the nation faced hard economic times, I was really becoming weary of asking people for money.

I'm sure most executive directors of nonprofit organizations have difficulties or disagreements with board members. Grandma's Marathon is governed by 17 individuals from our community, and, at times, I found myself in conflict with a few of them, tensions escalating.

I knew the marathon business well and I always vigorously fought to enhance the runner's experience at Grandma's. I strongly disliked when board members were more concerned with the bottom line than investing in our stakeholders.

Numerous times after a contentious lunch meeting with the executive committee I was overcome with severe stomach cramps. I would go home to bed, press a pillow to my abdomen and fall asleep.

In mid-April 2013, I made my mind up. I was going to announce my retirement to the board May 28, three weeks before our 37th Grandma's Marathon on June 22.

My decision was final. I came to the realization that I had to change things with my life. I was hoping to open up many doors and finally begin to smell the roses.

The 2013 Grandma's Marathon weekend would be the last time I would organize a race again. That was a promise I made to myself.

* * *

In 2011, I submitted a bid to the United States Track and Field (USATF) to host the men and women's half marathon national championships in 2012 and 2013. The Houston Marathon, which had been hosting the events for many years, won the bid for the 2012 Olympic Marathon Trials.

I felt we had a great opportunity to bring the nationals to Duluth, but the selection committee members were hell-bent to only award Grandma's Marathon the race in 2012. They were determined to give it back to Houston in 2013.

I called their bluff and pointed out that our proposal was for both years – not one. If they did not agree to both, I would withdraw our proposal altogether. The committee unanimously approved it and we were awarded the championships for both.

* * *

My retirement news spread quickly through the running community, and during the days leading to the race I was overcome numerous times with emotions. I can only describe it as overwhelming.

It was the perfect time to retire. I would complete my obligations to the championships. I had 37 wonderful years directing the race I started and loved. Many invited runners and USATF officials were in town.

I hinted to a few of my board members that I would prefer not to have a send-off party. I would rather have them make a donation in my name to Pancreatic Cancer Research, as two of our board members and numerous friends had perished from this horrible disease.

Tim Lee, a friend and board member, made an announcement at the beginning of the post-race banquet that Grandma's Marathon would be making a $5,000 donation to Pancreatic Cancer Research in my name. I was overwhelmed by the contribution and the standing ovation I received from the audience, including the 250 men and women who participated in the championships.

Kevin Pates from the Duluth News Tribune interviewed me at my home the next day and quoted me in the Monday paper:

"It was the most emotional day I've had in my life. When you leave something, you've started it's hard. I cried more tears than a human should. It was bittersweet, but certainly more sweet than bitter."

Pates also wrote, "Keenan's 37 years match the longest marathon tenure in the history of U.S. Road Racing with Boston Marathon's director, Will Cloney. The head man knew he reached the end of the run."

CHAPTER 33

Coaching Again

I have many fond memories in the 37-year journey with Grandma's Marathon. The most enjoyable part of my job was the personal interactions in the daily planning of our events.

Building relationships with sponsors, elite runners, attending volunteer committee meetings, working with law enforcement agencies; it was all fun. I loved planning.

The best part of my day, though, was at 11:30 a.m. when I took a short break and walked one block to Taste of Saigon for lunch. Owners, Hiep and Lan, had become dear friends years ago. I always felt I was part of their extended family. The food is great. I had my own table in the corner near the beer and soda cooler. If Hiep was around, he would take my order and dart into the kitchen and cook it with his special touch. My grandkids love going there as well. Of course, I had to make it a generational tradition.

The truth is, I still miss my marathon friends and if I am lucky we cross paths on occasion.

After retirement, I felt lost for a few months. After my wife left for work, I started cleaning closets and working on odd household chores. I lost my normal life routines.

I still had the desire to accomplish and create things. I soon started the Scott Keenan Consulting Company to help nonprofits and special events raise funds and become more effective in their communities.

I developed the Minnesuing Acres Women's Running Retreat in Lake Nebagamon, Wisconsin, which featured Kara Goucher and several other top-notch presenters. I was appointed the interim President and CEO for Visit Duluth, our convention and visitors bureau, and helped create a Sister Marathon Peace

Initiative comprised of 20 U.S. marathons with the country of Bhutan in Asia. I traveled to Reykjavik, Iceland, for the Midnight Sun Half Marathon, worked closely with the Duluth Library Foundation, and ran for County Commissioner, and lost.

Clearly, I was willing to do almost anything to keep busy.

On August 24, 2018, I received a call from Karen Stromme, the senior associate athletic director at the University of Minnesota Duluth. The women's cross-country coach had resigned, and they were in need of an interim coach for the season. I jumped out of my socks with elation and agreed to take the position immediately.

There was no mention of money at the time, but that wasn't important. What was paramount was I was going to be a coach again. The last time I coached was 28 years earlier at the College of St. Scholastica.

Josh Berlo, UMD's athletic director, made it official at lunch on August 27. On the same day, at 3 p.m., I was introduced to the 17 varsity women runners as the new head coach.

This was one day before my 65th birthday. It was the greatest present I could have ever received.

Our first meet was September 6 at the Nemadji Golf Course in Superior, Wisconsin, the Dan Conway Classic 5K. I had just 10 days to prepare.

We hadn't had a practice yet, I didn't know their names, and I had no clue about their running backgrounds or personalities. The coach who recruited the team would not be there.

This was far from an ideal situation and it was certainly going to be a difficult challenge. I had confidence in my coaching philosophies and training strategies, but first of all we needed to get to know each other.

I scheduled one-on-one meetings with each of the runners in my small office on the second floor of the UMD Sports and Health Center. For some reason it smelled like mustard all of the time, even after they painted it. I was grateful for the window.

I put my framed picture of Steve Prefontaine and me on the office countertop next to my desk. I was thinking it wouldn't hurt to establish a little credibility right away. The team was impressed, and it became the opening for us to get to know each other. Soon, members of the men's team were stopping by to take a look.

I added three walk-on runners, bringing the squad to 20 women. In my mind, that was the perfect number.

We were a young team, mostly freshmen and sophomores, a few juniors and one senior. At my introduction meeting I promised I would give a 100 percent effort each day and all I asked was for them to do the same. I also told them I was planning to undertrain them. We would focus on quality workouts vs. quantity, allowing for fresh legs for races.

I never wanted to be a coach who pushed too hard and over trained athletes. It was more important to get them to the starting line instead of the sidelines.

Much of my effort was to teach how to race efficiently and wisely. One of my sayings which I repeated often – You can never win the race in the first mile, but you could lose it.

I was fortunate to have Taylor Nystrom, the director of ticket sales and operations at UMD, as my assistant coach. She was a talented UMD runner a few years earlier. We clicked immediately and she provided a tremendous amount of training knowledge and handled the administrative responsibilities. It was a welcomed partnership for our three months together.

I was extremely nervous on race day in Superior, but I was impressed with the work ethic and athletic abilities of each runner. They were ready to be tested.

It was a great afternoon for the Bulldogs. We placed nine runners in the top 10. Morgan Radel, a talented freshman, won the race.

In the paper the next day, Duluth News Tribune Sportswriter, Louis St. George III wrote: "Keenan was plenty animated during the race. He resembled a kid on Christmas morning bouncing over to congratulate race winner, Radel, and each member of his team. His ever-present smile and enthusiasm for coaching was on full display."

I was excited alright, but mostly I was proud of our runners. On the short bus ride back to the campus, I stood up and told them, "We are now a team…congratulations."

UMD's 2018 Women's Cross-Country Team. Coach Taylor Nystrom (left) and Coach Scott Keenan (right). Photo Credit: UMD Athletics

* * *

Going back to 1982, my women's cross-country team at the College of St. Scholastica finished second in our nine state NCAA Division III regional meet. The top two teams qualified to run in the national championships in Fredonia, New York.

We were not considered by the pollsters to finish in the top 50 percent at regions. In fact, I am almost sure most coaches had no clue where St. Scholastica was. This was probably one of the greatest surprises in the region.

One week later in Upstate New York we finished 10th in the nation (NCAA Division III).

Early in the season at UMD, the St. Scholastica Athletic Department notified me that my 1982 team and I would be inducted into their Athletic Hall of Fame. Unfortunately, the timing was bad. I had to travel to Grand Forks, North Dakota for a meet on the night of the banquet. The St. Scholastica team forgave me, but only because I was coaching again.

I did record a video congratulating the St. Scholastica team on the award, telling them how proud I was.

On my bus ride to Grand Forks, my new team played a video they produced congratulating me for my Hall of Fame induction at CSS, which was another emotional moment for me.

On our return trip to Duluth, we stopped at Dick and Jill Beardsley's Bed and Breakfast in Bemidji, Minnesota. Dick told many stories and signed autographs for the team members.

* * *

I thought it was important to have another one-on-one session with my UMD runners before we traveled to the Division II regional meet in Joplin, Missouri. It was time to reflect on the year and establish goals for the last race of the season. I shared with them the Hall of Fame plaque I received from St. Scholastica, which included a picture of the 12 runners on the team. I said this group was always considered the underdog, but it didn't matter, as they ignored it and kept improving each week.

The UMD team was young but ran as veterans and always gave 100 percent. During the season we won three meets. On November 7 we finished seventh in the NCAA Division II Regional Meet out of 35 schools.

We were not considered to be in the top 15 in the pre-race rankings. Our team collectively passed 120 competitors in the final three kilometers. They had learned the importance of pacing.

The season was an emotional time. I was grateful for the opportunity to coach again and help these 20 women become better runners. Our seventh-place finish surprised a lot of people. They were very proud of their accomplishment and I couldn't have been more proud of them for never giving up. This team surprised the world in so many ways.

During the last team photo at regionals, I was given a water bottle drenching. I became overwhelmed with the gesture. My time at UMD was an experience of a lifetime and I'll never forget it.

Thank you, Megan, Elizabeth, Tayler, Kyes, Kathryn, REE (two thumbs up and a smile), Lexie, Mason, Morgan, Haleigh, Alex, Allison, Gabi, Isabel, Taylor, Mackenzie, Elayna, Teresa, Isabelle, Lauren, and Coach Nystrom.

You deeply enriched my life!

NCAA Division II Regional Meet in Joplin, Missouri.

* * *

On my final day at UMD, tears welled up in my eyes as I was carrying my box of coaching materials to my truck. I was sad. My coaching experience was the revival I needed. It gave me new and welcomed purpose. I felt I made a difference to these young athletes, even if it was in a small way.

The memories of coaching this wonderful team will certainly last the rest of my life. It is hard to explain and impossible to describe in words the joy I received from them.

In the back of my mind, I felt there was a good chance UMD would bring me back as an assistant coach. As I look back now, it was wishful thinking on my part. My dream of continuing with UMD athletics was slipping away as the weeks passed.

* * *

On May 7, 2019, I received another call from UMD to help organize the Northern Sun Intercollegiate Conference (NSIC) Outdoor Track and Field Championships. The events would be held on UMD's campus May 10.

I was in disbelief with the short notice but accepted immediately because I was definitely willing to help my alma mater.

On May 8, during the early morning hours, a huge wintery storm left more than ten inches of heavy snow in Duluth. This was the largest amount of snow recorded in May since 1884.

Thursday morning, with my winter boots on, I brought my shovel and squeegee to the track to begin snow removal. The snow was melting quickly with the warmer afternoon temps, but the workload was still immense. The track was cleared by 6 p.m. that day.

At this point, I was hoping to continue coaching somewhere. During the conference track meet I bumped into Dave Wicker, a good friend and former teammate of mine at UMD.

Wicker is the head track and cross-country coach at East High School in Duluth.

I mentioned that if he ever had an opening for an assistant coach, I would love to help. I felt it wouldn't hurt to begin planting the seed for coaching at the high school level.

In mid-July 2019, Coach Wicker knocked on my door and explained that one of his cross-country coaches was having knee replacement surgery and would be unavailable that fall.

I was still hanging onto the thinnest thread of hope I'd be offered an assistant coaching position at UMD, so Dave gave me until August 1 to make a decision. My wish to stay involved at UMD didn't work out, and I accepted the coaching position at East.

It was a dream come true. The only fear I had was learning more than 100 names. This was certainly a challenge for my 66-year-old mind.

This would be another interim position, but I didn't mind. I was coaching again and as happy as I could be.

The 2019 season was rewarding in many ways. I found that coaches can really make a difference on how young athletes embrace running. The theme was simple. Run for fun, enjoy the journey.

The 2020 season was quite different and difficult. My wife and I both decided to take a very cautious approach to the devastating COVID-19 pandemic.

In early summer, coach Wicker asked if I was willing to continue coaching. Coach Shonda Peller, one of the three coaches, was moving to Florida. I was beaming with excitement about the offer but knew Carrie would not be thrilled. I was waiting for the perfect time to break the news to her.

The perfect time wasn't so perfect. I will just say it was a challenging moment. I didn't have to beg, but I was prepared to do so. I promised to follow all of the strict safety protocols. I wouldn't ride on the school buses or enter school buildings. I would wear a mask at all times and keep more than six feet apart from runners and coaches.

I appreciated the opportunity to be a part of the coaching staff at East High School. My love for coaching was once again brought to the forefront.

We had more than 100 boys and girls on the 2020 team from seventh to 12th graders. They were fantastic and dedicated runners who wanted to improve. Their enthusiasm and spirit were exhilarating. Early in the season they understood the importance of team, and that individual accolades would come later.

At the Section 7AA meet in Princeton, Minnesota, our boys and girls finished second out of 16 schools. They ran their best race of the season and qualified for the state meet. Unfortunately, there was no state meet because of the virus.

It was a great season, and I am so proud of both teams. It was another life experience that I will never forget.

Legends of Our Sport

Spreading the word about Grandma's Marathon was a high priority for me. Our annual advertising budget was minuscule, and we needed to find other ways to market our race. Bringing legends of our sport to Grandma's Marathon helped develop important credibility and we hoped they would tell our story to the world.

The word-of-mouth was becoming a success story that heightened our national popularity. We were developing loyal friendships and ambassadors across the country.

Maybe, in a small way, I was also boosting my ego by being associated with my running heroes. Over the years, four Olympic gold medalists joined us and shared their stories with the runners and the media.

Jess Koski, Jay Lee, Scott Keenan, Lasse Viren, Luc Waegeman, Kirk Jewell, and Camille Waegeman

Billy Mills – United States – 1964 10,000-meter gold medalist in Tokyo, Japan.

Frank Shorter – United States – 1972 marathon gold medalist in Munich, West Germany.

Lasse Viren – Finland – four-time gold medalist – 1972 5,000 & 10,000 meters in Munich, West Germany; 1976 5,000 & 10,000 meters in Montreal, Quebec.

Joan Benoit – United States – 1984 marathon gold medalist in Los Angeles.

A list of some of the other running legends who have been guests at Grandma's Marathon:

Arthur Lydiard, Hal Higdon, Derek Clayton, Kathrine Switzer, Roger Robinson, Priscilla Welch, Alex Ratelle, Fred Lebow, Garry Bjorklund, Francie Larrieu Smith, Jeff Galloway, Anne Audain, Bill Squires, Dr. David Martin, Bill Rodgers, Dick Beardsley, Lorraine Moller, Jim Ryan, Barney and Janis Klecker, Ron Daws, Cathy O'Brien, Dr. Jack Scaff, Doug Kurtis, Dr. Joan Ullyot, John Campbell, Michael Pinocci, Lynn Jennings, Gayle Barron, Tommy Leonard, Deena Kastor, Bill Dellinger, Jon Sinclair, Michele Lilienthal, Benji Durden, Suzy Favor Hamilton, Jane Welzel, Craig Virgin, Marla Runyan, Mark Conover, Grete Waitz, J.D. Denton, Patti Catalano-Dillon, Antonio Vega, Don Kardong, Kara Goucher, Joe Henderson, Jenny Spangler, Katie McGee, Jerry Lynch, Dr. Mona Shangold, Dr. Peter Wood, Pete Pfitzinger, Dan Conway, George Sheehan, Margaret Groos, John Parker, Sister Marion Irvine, Kenny Moore, Lisa Dorfman, Jonathan Beverly, Gordon Bakoulis, Candace Karu, Andrew Carlson, Carrie Tollefson, Ryan Meissen and Katie McGregor.

I apologize if I missed any of our legends. These individuals have been an important part of our marathon history. I challenge readers to do research on their contributions to running. They have made a tremendous difference to the sport we love.

10 Life Tidbits of Scott Keenan

1. In March of 1993, I married my wife, Carrie, at the age of 39 ½. I previously read somewhere if you didn't marry before age 40, the chances of getting married is less than 5%. I started to seriously look for a lifelong mate when I was 37. Thank you, Carrie, for the many years of your enduring patience and love.

2. I have six wonderful grandchildren who have been an indispensible part of my personal growth. It is impossible to express the love and joy they have provided to me over the years. Thank you, Krystal, Austin, Aaron, Andrew, Skylar and Ariena. I truly love each and every one of you...Grandpa Scott.

3. I served eight years on the Duluth City Council from 1992 – 1999. I was selected by my peers to be president of the council in 1995 and 1999. I enjoyed every minute of my tenure and quickly learned the most important part of being an elected official is representing your constituents, not your own personal biases and agenda. It was one of the most rewarding periods of my life.

4. My baby brother, James Robert Keenan, passed away as an infant on December 1, 1954. It was a painful memory for my mother, and she kept it a secret from everyone, including her children. I found out I had another brother when I was sixteen and was in complete shock. I visit him every year at the cemetery to clean his gravestone and say a prayer.

5. In the fall of 1971, while grouse hunting with my friend, Ricky Brown, we became lost in the remote northwoods near Brimson, Minnesota. As we tried to sleep in the woods that night, we could hear the wolves howling near our

camp. It ended up being a 30-hour survival experience and finally Ricky's brother, David, rescued us. The Duluth News Tribune wrote a paragraph about it saying that two lost hunters were found okay near Brimson. They were just cold and hungry.

6. In the summer of 1969, at the age of 15, I was on the Red Sox Babe Ruth baseball team in the Duluth Heights neighborhood. It was the last game of the season for our league, and I was patiently sitting on the pine bench hoping to get into the game. In the bottom of the ninth inning, coach Jack House called my name as a pinch runner for my teammate on third base.

   Everyone on both teams knew House had a plan for me to steal home. After a fake attempt, hoping the catcher would throw wildly back to third base, the play would now be on. As the pitcher was in his windup, I sprinted as fast as I could to home plate and stopped three feet in front of the catcher, with the ball in his mitt. I turned back and started to run to third and counted one, two and three as the ball whistled by my left ear. I quickly turned again and slid safely into home to win the game. Our team now was heading to the Minneapolis metro area for the state tournament. Baseball is still my favorite sport today.

7. I didn't realize when I was married in 1993 that I would dig up half of our backyard for flower gardens. Where we live, inches below the topsoil, there is nothing but solid red Lake Superior clay. Replacing a foot of the clay with black garden dirt is certainly a time-consuming project. It would be one garden per year. A wheelbarrow and a shovel would be my best friends. I soon stopped complaining and became an amateur gardener myself, but I still take directions from my wife's expertise. Over the years we have been included in numerous city-wide garden tours. The gardens now

include a pond and a 30-foot river with thousands of Lake Superior field stone rocks lining the riverbed and pond.

8. I have always loved listening to music – it makes me happy. Many years ago, my wife bought me the best present ever, an outdoor "Rock Speaker" which we wired into my almost-vintage 1984 CD console. Now I am able to listen to my 400+ CD collection while landscaping and working in the gardens. Just maybe Carrie had it figured out that this was a good way to keep me working outside all day.

   My top 15 favorite music artists and bands:
   1. Doors
   2. Jayhawks
   3. Alabama Shakes
   4. John Lennon
   5. The Cranberries
   6. Neil Young
   7. Soul Asylum
   8. Garry Puckett & the Union Gap
   9. Traveling Wilburys
   10. Sinead O'Connor
   11. Neko Case
   12. Lucy Michelle and the Velvet Lapelles
   13. B-52's
   14. Hana Rae Beale
   15. Dazyhead Mazey

9. In 1986, my friend, Don Wicklund, introduced me to red wine. It definitely was an acquired taste for me, but I was intrigued by the complexities of the different grape varieties. I loved the aromas, the nose and then the taste.

   Within a year, I had 50 bottles stacked awkwardly in a cool and dark back portion of my basement. It was a perfect place to store wine. I read in a wine magazine that if you were going to become a collector you needed to have a minimum of 50 bottles and a good variety of different types. Over the years, I have asked a lot of questions of experts and I read a lot of wine magazines. I developed a deep appreciation for all kinds of wine.

   I started purchasing wine that my budget allowed but were worthy of collecting and storing for years. As my personal finances increased, I purchased more expensive wines and joined many wine clubs. I have traveled to California and Oregon wine country many times. Today, I have a cellar of over 500 bottles and they are still stacked awkwardly in the back portion of my basement. I often use my favorite motto: *A good bottle of wine will make any day a special occasion.*

10. When I was a young boy, I found an Evening Grosbeak with a broken wing in our neighborhood woods. I brought it home, and the bird became a part of our family for over a decade.

    I have always enjoyed watching birds, and it became a passion of mine after I built the pond and river in our backyard. The fresh running water and all of the vegetation has created a natural habitat that attracts many different species.

One of the most memorable moments of bird watching was when approximately 300 Bohemian Waxwings were on their spring migration north when they decided to pick clean my crabapple tree. I watched motionlessly for an hour, witnessing how they took turns, a hundred at a time, devouring the apples. Countless birds have visited our property and it has certainly been a joy watching and studying their movements.

Scott Keenan Recognition Awards

2018 – College of Saint Scholastica Athletic Hall of Fame

2014 – Grandma's Marathon Hall of Fame

2014 – Running USA Hall of Champions

2014 – USATF Minnesota Lifetime Contribution Award

2014 – Event Director College Hall of Fame

2013 – USATF Women's Long Distance Running Marja Bakker Contributor of the Year Award

2008 – USATF Allan Steinfeld Award

2008 – Portland Marathon Event Director Professor of the Year Award

2005 – USATF Minnesota Hall of Fame

2003 – Road Race Management Race Director of the Year Award

2003 – Portland Marathon Event Director Conference Race Director of the Year Award

1986 – Minnesota Distance Running Association Distinguished Service Award

Letter from Andy Borg, president of Grandma's, Inc, after 1996 Marathon

June 24, 1996

Scott Keenan
Grandma's Marathon
P O Box 16234
Duluth, MN 55816

Scott...

...Who would have ever thought as you and I and George sat in my office up above the old Saloon & Deli that what we discussed would result in what we both experienced last week. ***WOW!***

On Friday, I had the opportunity to attend, I know a dream of yours, the Expo. It's starting, Scott, and it's going to be real big! I'm sure the Expo is going to grow into a huge event. The Spaghetti Feed...what a phenomenal organization! Scott, we would've never been able to do that one in the tent. I can't imagine how much spaghetti was served. And just to think, all those revenues for the next year's event!

The Irvin 5K...I had a chance to watch the finish, along with a heck of a lot of other people. What a great event. People standing on the Irvin, people lining the streets. It looked like a Marathon finish. What an exciting event!

Friday night's entertainment in the tent...a real WOW! The tent was packed, the midway was packed, our operations were packed. Scott, a real success!

And needless to say, Saturday...ahhhh! Pulled off the race without a hitch. Once again, great volunteers, tremendous organization.

People just couldn't believe the course, the activity on the course, the people lining the course. Scott, what a tremendous effort!

And then you guys were able to pull off the weather change. Great running weather in the morning, great relaxing weather in the afternoon, and a tremendous opportunity on Saturday night. I went through the midway, the tent, caught a little bit of Molly and the Heymakers. Great band, great crowd, and hopefully tremendous sales for the Marathon!

Scott, a sincere thank you for the awards they bestowed on Mick and myself. The only face that was missing, in my opinion, on the Wall of Fame is yours. And hopefully, they'll reserve a spot right next to Mick and me where your face will appear shortly. I'm sure it's politics and when you decide in 30 years to turn the directorship over to one of your protégés, they'll probably make the award then.

In the interim, however, a number of the 20-year Grandma's employees got together and bought you a little gift to show you our appreciation for all that you've done for our Grandma's organization the last 20 years. Scott, you and Grandma's Marathon mean a lot to us employees at Grandma's Restaurant.

The last ten years have been a wonderful ten years. You and the board of directors have made phenomenal strides on improving the entire event. And you and I both know <u>*you've*</u> *been the driving force. Scott, without you the race would've faded away. Your drive and your persistence have made the event what it is today.*

As I've stated in the past, Scott, I'm very, very proud of you. You've accomplished much since we first met some 20 years ago...Scott, you've been persistent in making it the best runner's race in the country. And you've also allowed a little activity before the race and after the race. But you've never lost focus on making sure each and every runner has a red carpet rolled out for them each time they participate in the event.

I saw your dad on Saturday afternoon out in front of Angie's. I haven't seen him for many years, Scott. We had to reminisce about how we used to store all the stuff in his yard, how you started out using his phone number. He was pretty proud, Scott, of you, the race, and your other accomplishments. It was great to have chatted with him and laughed about how far the race has come over the last 20 years…

Scott, my congratulations on another exceptional event, on 20 years of phenomenal accomplishment, and now let's get on with the next ten so we can reminisce at our 30th. Myself and the Grandma's organization are always behind you 100%. Just keep me advised where we can be of assistance.

Sincerely yours,

Andy

Written by the Duluth News Tribune Editorial Board and published on Friday, June 21, 2013

Our View/2013 Grandma's

End of an era at end of marathon

Grandma's Marathon will never be the same. Not after this year's running. That's because Scott Keenan, the heart and soul of the marathon for all of its 37 years, the behind-the-scenes driving force, the one who pulled it off and got it done year after year, and one of Grandma's original founders, is stepping away. He made the announcement earlier this month, telling his staff first: After tomorrow's race, consider him retired.

And put an exclamation point on an incredible run – and on his hold as the longest-serving marathon race director in the U.S.

"There's been a turning point for me the last three years," Keenan, 59, told the News Tribune's Kevin Pates, himself an icon of the marathon retiring after this year's race. "When I've left the house each morning of the race I've told my wife that it was my last year. It's been on my mind, and this year I finally decided it was in my best interest to move on. It's hard to let go, but I'm not willing to take that stress anymore."

That stress: Keenan has been the guy in charge every year of nearly 6,000 volunteers; of more than 17,000 runners, some of them from among the ranks of the world's best and fastest; of a $2.39 million annual budget; and of an annual $8.5 million economic impact on the Duluth community.

Grandma's is Minnesota's oldest marathon and long was the state's largest after Keenan and his North Shore Striders, a local running club, started the race in 1977. Keenan was still in college then at the University of Minnesota Duluth and was still painting houses to make a real living. He became the marathon's full-time director in the mid-1980s. His commitment – always, and more than achieved – has been to make sure Grandma's is one of the world's elite marathons.

It's also a can't-miss-late-June moment on every Duluthians' calendar.

"You feel like everyone in town is involved in the marathon," course record holder and Minnesota native Dick Beardsley, 57, said from home in Austin, Texas, in a phone interview with Pates this month. "I don't know how you can do it any better."

The Northland and all the running world can send Keenan off with gratitude, admiration and appreciation.

We can also thank and pay tribute to Pates, who covered every Grandma's Marathon but the inaugural one. He wrote about the race even while running it on five occasions. Pates was inducted into the Grandma's Marathon Hall of Fame in 2010.

"Some of the most inspiring stories are those of your neighbor, or brother, sister, mom or dad. They set a goal, train and get to the finish," Pates wrote this month. "That's what makes marathoning special."

Icons like Scott Keenan – and Pates – make marathoning special, too. An arms-in-the-air, ribbon-breaking salute to both of them.

Editors

I want to give a special thanks to my editors for your many hours of hard work. The book would never have been possible without you.

Kevin Pates

Kevin Pates spent 40 years in the journalism business, the last 35 as a sports writer for the Duluth News Tribune. He grew up in St. Paul, was a 1973 college of St. Thomas graduate and worked for the News Tribune from 1978 – 2013. He ran in Grandma's Marathon five times in the early 1980s, wrote about the race for 35 years, and completed 26 marathons in all.

Laura Bergen

Laura Bergen has been involved with Grandma's Marathon since 1999, starting as an intern during the spring of her senior year at the University of Minnesota Duluth. In March of 2000, while living the ski bum life in Crested Butte, Colorado, Scott, much to the relief of Laura's parents, hired her as the marathon's public relations director. Twenty years and multiple positions within the organization later, Laura is currently the registration and expo director for Grandma's Marathon. She lives in Duluth with her husband, Patrick, and their three children – Margaret, Max and Hazel.

Carolyn and Jerry Zanko

Carolyn and Jerry Zanko have been running since the 1970's and ran their first Grandma's Marathon in 1984. They also volunteered for many local races, including the Garry Bjorklund Half Marathon and Grandma's Marathon. They have run in Maui's Hana Relay, as members of a team, with their final race in 2017. They have been married since 1981.

Chris Gillespie is the author of *Gracerunner: A Running Book and One of Faith.* I consider Chris to be a good friend, but a person I barely know. In Chapter 9 of his book, his words of wisdom always resonate with me:

"Never allow your circumstances to dictate your character, but rather allow your character to show through in your circumstances."

Thank you, Chris Gillespie.

Have a good night everyone and remember –
Live your life to the fullest!

Made in the USA
Middletown, DE
23 May 2021